And Now For Something Completely Different...
...Living Life to the Full

Keith Mills

First published in Great Britain in 2023
Copyright © Keith Mills 2023
Published by Victor Publishing - victorpublishing.co.uk

Keith Mills has asserted his right under the Copyright, Designs and Patents Act 1988 to be identified as the author of this work.

All rights reserved. No part of this publication may be reproduced, distributed, or transmitted in any form or by any means, including photocopying, recording, or other electronic or mechanical methods, without the prior written permission of the author.

Every reasonable effort has been made to trace copyright holders of material reproduced in this book, but if any have been inadvertently overlooked, the author would be glad to hear from them.

ISBN: 9798864102084

And Now For Something Completely Different ...
...Living Life to the Full

Keith Mills

For everybody who has made our life
what it has become

And Now For Something Completely Different... ...living life to the full

Contents

1. War Baby 7
2. A Marple Childhood... 15
3. On to Grammar School 21
4. And on from school... 27
5. A Minisink Summer - USA 1964 37
6. Zambia 51
7. Rogan's first safari 73
8. Uganda - The Koboko Years... 79
9. Uganda - Life under Amin 97
10. Back to England..111
11. From High Lane to Argentina 119
12. A Silver Wedding Purchase.. 125
13. Football and all that 131
14. Taking Early Retirement 149
15. The Call of the Boards 153
16. Making the Move... 163
17. The France Years.. 169
18. Back to Uganda and Les Amis d'Ouganda................ 183
19. After All These Years 197
20. And Finally.. 205

And Now For Something Completely Different... ...living life to the full

And Now For Something Completely Different... ...living life to the full

Chapter 1

War Baby

Mum and Dad met at New Mills Dramatic & Operatic Society sometime in the mid to late 1930s. There they performed in musicals such as "Rose Marie" and "Katinka". For anybody who knew them, that will seem entirely appropriate. Dad was a consummate entertainer by nature and small kids always loved their "Uncle Bill". Friends regularly laughed at his renditions of Stanley Holloway monologues, and he could sing well and play the piano by ear. In the 1950s, every home seemed to have a piano and Dad entertained the guests with great panache.

As a normally rather reserved, diffident man in "real life", he came into his own when people were there to be entertained. And Mum? She always loved the limelight and she never tired of telling how she won the "best legs" competition when she worked as a secretary at Bredbury Steelworks which, oddly enough, was called Exors of James Mills. As far as I am aware, there was no family connection.

Although Dad was born in Venado Tuerto, Argentina, he came from a High Lane family which is where he was brought up. From the Horse Shoe Inn, the family moved to Bank House on the canal bridge and finally to "Venado" on Carr Brow. Mum was brought up in Failsworth and when her parents moved to Disley, "grangran" Keating set up a bakery and shop business in a small terraced property. Eva and Bill were married at St Mary's Church in Disley on 30th December 1939 and spent their early years together at "Hill View", Mum's parents' home. How everyone fitted in to this tiny house is a real mystery.

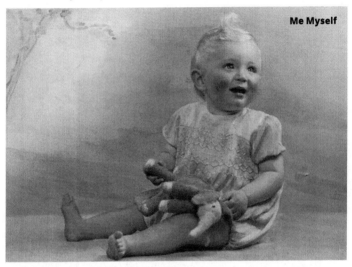

Me Myself

Nevertheless, I was born there on 5th August 1942 and delivered by Dr Titcombe who lived in the big house across the road. Truly a war baby; at the time, dad was working as an electrician on the Lancaster Bombers which were being manufactured at the Woodford factory. Mum worked on nursing and care duties at Lyme Hall which housed refugee children; each morning she walked across Disley and Lyme Park to work. It was quite appropriate really because, although her parents had vetoed the idea, she had always wanted to be a nurse.

The front room at Hill View housed the shop, selling bread, cakes, tobacco products and sweets. The bakery

And Now For Something Completely Different... ...living life to the full

itself was in the cellar where grangran spent almost all of his time. I remember virtually nothing about the first few years of my life apart from a memory of a German V2 rocket passing over on its way down in nearby New Mills, and we all had to crowd into the cellar to watch it pass. Or do I remember it? Perhaps it is something that has passed down in folk memory. But I think I do.

Most of my early memories come from after we had moved to a "semi" at 14 Norwood Avenue, High Lane. We had moved there by the time that my younger brother, Kevin, was born, on June 13th 1944. We still spent a lot of time at Nanna's place. We would walk there through Disley woods along the A6 which in those days was a quiet, safe route. I remember Kevin in his pram as we shuffled through the Autumn leaves, while I searched out the conkers that covered the footpath and embankments.

Just up the road from the shop was Len Travis, the coalman, who delivered his goods on a cart pulled by his horse, Dobbin. Certainly there was a lot of competition to gather up the horse's droppings to manure the gardens.

The village highlight of the year in those days was Disley Wakes, the annual funfair. I wonder if the legend is true that traditionally it was held on the second weekend after the first snow? Certainly by this time it was a November fixture and we loved it; riding the cocks and hens and knocking over coconuts and tin cans to win a goldfish that never seemed to survive the month. Grangran's brandy-snaps were another tradition for the village; he made them especially for the festival and they sold like hot cakes (really).

Postwar life was not easy with its ration book restrictions, though black market specials could sometimes be

And Now For Something Completely Different... ...living life to the full

gained, with occasional treats for the children after a walk to the grocery shop at the other end of the village. Later, in more affluent times, Mum still would not eat rabbit. She remembered it as wartime poor folks' fare.

Throughout her life, mum loved parties. Kevin and I used to sit at the top of the stairs listening to a cacophony of women crying their eyes out over their doses of gin, known then as mothers' ruin. I cannot now for the life of me understand what pleasure we children got from draining the dregs from the beer bottles the next morning; I suppose that it made us feel grown-up.

I recall one unpleasant bus journey back from Disley to High Lane. In those days the cross pieces on the lamp posts pointed out into the road, not parallel to it, a much safer position. The bus pulled up at the gates to Lyme Park and one of them went straight through the upstairs window, severely injuring the people sitting there. I cannot remember how long it was before we got home as the driver sped non-stop to Stepping Hill Hospital in Stockport. An unpleasant event surely, but a great adventure for us.

I went to High Lane Primary School (it later became a Thai restaurant). It was only a short walk down the avenue and round the corner to the front entrance, but in case of dire need, there was a way to escape being punished for being late; at the bottom of our garden was a wall over which we could clamber directly into the playground and save this guilty party from a caned hand.

Was I a good pupil? I've no idea, but I doubt it. Throughout my school years, all my reports said the

And Now For Something Completely Different... ...living life to the full

same thing: "Keith talks too much"; but I do recall the wonderful pleasure of being able to take the class hamsters home for the school holidays.

There were not too many day-out treats but on one occasion it was planned to go to see the planes at Ringway Airport. Dad regularly worked from home; he was in the process of setting up as a self-employed auto-electrician. Throughout our childhood, our days out and even holidays, were often delayed or even cancelled when somebody turned up for repairs to be urgently made so that they (the customers) could get away for their period of relaxation. On this occasion, the object was a motor bike. The repairs were completed, but it was my foolishness that led to a wasted day for the whole family. To check whether all was well, I grasped the exhaust firmly. It was still fiendishly hot and my shrieks must have been audible across the village as I lost several layers of skin. Ah well, another lesson learned the hard way.

It was during these years that Mum suffered from pleurisy. The prescription was isolation and fresh air and she was sent to a sanatorium at Market Drayton in Shropshire. There was no doubt that Dad was unable to care for two young children and earn the family living at the same time, so we were shipped out to family and friends. Kevin went to Oldham to be looked after by Uncle and Auntie Mac (Alec & Irene McMillan), our godparents. Irene had been a childhood friend of Mum back in Failsworth. She had come up in the world with Alec who now owned several Lancashire factories producing "Latafoam" mattresses and related products.

I went to the family of another old friend of Mum's (Joyce Milner as she was then) whose dad was a Disley plumber. The primary school was only just across the road and my early love of reading had already developed because my main memory of the place was the great joy I felt when the library box was delivered each Friday afternoon.

We had a nasty experience during this time when the brakes on Gordon Brooke's car (Joyce Milner's boyfriend) failed and we careered into a high brick wall between Disley and High Lane. The vehicle turned on its side and we were trapped until enough glass had been cleared away to enable us to climb through the side window. I guess we could not have been too injured as I have no recollection of being hospitalised.

During the school holidays, I was sent to Wallasey to stay with Nana Mills, Dad's Mum, and with Auntie Wynne, his "little" sister, and her husband Uncle Stan. Those were happy times; it was only a couple of minutes walk down to the prom where we could play on the beach and watch all the big ships on the Mersey. We would walk along the river to New Brighton and all the fun of the fair; it was a lively resort in those days and of course we loved

At Wallasey

the fairgrounds and its crowds. The pier was another attraction and we could take the ferry from there to Liverpool where we would enjoy a ride on the overhead

And Now For Something Completely Different... ...living life to the full

railway through the docks, sail back to Seacombe and then home on one of the pea-green buses. I got myself into real trouble when the family sent me for one of the promenade photographers. I misunderstood and had my own photograph taken with my bucket and spade. That was an extravagant expense when the whole family should have been snapped for the price!

It was after Mum's return home from the sanatorium that their best friends, Joyce and Gordon, married at the same Disley church, just ten years after Mum and Dad's wedding. Yours truly was recruited as a seven-year-old page boy with a neighbour, June Lever, a year my senior, as bridesmaid. I am pretty sure that her dress was more comfortable than my draughty kilt; but yes, despite the ribbing that came in abundant supply, I did wear something underneath it!

One other life altering event happened to me at this time when I was taken by Gordon and his brother Basil to watch Stockport County at Edgeley Park. We stood (you always did in those days) in the shed at what is today the Cheadle End. I remember little of the game, who the opponents were, or who won but it was so exciting as a six-year-old to be present at the big ground. My only recollection of play at all was yelling for a penalty, but I suspect that it was not given. What is certain is that a lifelong addiction had been set up.

Apart from the occasional day trip to Blackpool, holidays were a week in North Wales. The first post-war excursion was in a bungalow at Llanbedrog and of course it rained almost all week. At least we learned how to play cards; stop the cab and 21. There was nothing else to do apart from the few occasions when the mists lifted and allowed us to get out and hare around the beach.

And Now For Something Completely Different... ...living life to the full

Chapter 2

A Marple Childhood

In 1949 we moved two miles down the road to 85 Hibbert Lane, Marple. Our new home was the top one of a row of newly-built council houses. Because of its situation, it was where all the lorries entered the site to drop off the building materials, we had the biggest of all the gardens; plenty of room for cricket and football. The brick wall was whitewashed and quickly became dirty. So we should have to do some painting ourselves shouldn't we? Of course not; the responsibility for upkeep belonged to Marple Urban District Council and tenants were not allowed to do anything for themselves. We had to wait our turn which did not come round very often.

New Brighton Pier with Mum, Dad, Nan Mills and brother Kevin

An earth footpath and then a hedge separated our garden from the road. Later, after the hedge had been ripped out and a proper footpath had been laid, dad wanted to bring the car into the garden. Not a chance - that would mean lowering the kerb and making a gap in the wall and the

And Now For Something Completely Different... ...living life to the full

council would not permit that. For many years to come our car (a 1934 Standard 8) remained on the roadside or in the garage hired from the Braddock family across the road.

Hibbert Lane and the area around it was at that time an ideal, rural place to be brought up. There was minimal traffic. I say that advisedly. A neighbour's dog, Chopper, was a blind spaniel who used to lie in the middle of the road oblivious to what little traffic there was. Cars had to drive round him all day until his mistress came home from work. When she got off the bus a good 200 yards down the road, he could not see her, but he knew her footstep and he was off to meet her.

It was an idyllic spot for young children. Nowadays from the rear of "85" all the way up to All Saints Church on the Ridge is filled up with row after row of houses on both sides of the canal. In those days there wasn't a single building. There was so much space to wander and play at will. It was only a ten minute walk into Marple village, but there were two farms between us and the shops. Hollands where we romped around the fields and woods with their son, David, and Cote Bridge Farm, which was on the bend on the other side of Hibbert Lane and where there are now bungalows and more council houses.

Memories of childhood at this stage of my life can be divided between school and play; less of the former, more of the latter!

Between "85" and the canal bridge was the croft, an open space with a tree in the middle which doubled as a chalked cricket wicket in summer and a goalpost, partnered with our coats, in winter. There was bags of room for hide and seek, catch and kiss and of course the always enjoyable "cowboys and indians'. We died and were resurrected dozens of times a day during the holidays. Another more leisurely pleasure was fishing in the canal. There was a warm water outlet from the Goyt Mill just by the bridge which attracted the fish and made our success rate much higher than it otherwise would have been. If we went further afield, there were adventures galore up at the quarry, a beautiful place itself with views over the valley and across to Mellor on the other side. Then in winter there was sledging. We could speed all the way down from the Ridge almost as far as the main road itself. What space we had! On the bridge itself was Carringtons, the bakers who provided sweets when the "gang" needed a break and for meals to take home with their pies and cakes.

School was All Saints C of E Primary on Brick Bridge Road , a 15 minute walk from home either along Mount Drive (the Ecclesbridge estate did not exist at that time) or, as we preferred, along the canal towpath. I say 15 minutes, but at that age you don't walk briskly in a straight line do you? Which meant of course that we were regularly late for registration, even though we knew the punishment. Mr Higson was head when I first attended and he was replaced by Mr Martlow. Which was the one (or was it both of them?) who lined us up behind a white line to wait until he came along to cane the hand of each one of us in turn. To receive this punishment was a badge of honour rather than a deterrent.

That was the soft punishment, much to be preferred to the buckle end of the belt that hung behind our kitchen door. That was a true deterrent, a fearful and painful strap that was always wielded by Mum. Dad was the protector, not the punisher.

Nearly all the staff at that time were unmarried ladies. I remember two in particular, both of whom lived almost on the doorstep of the school. We understood that Miss Brown's boyfriend or fiancé left for the war and that was the end of her marriage prospects. There always seemed to be a surfeit of unmarried women (from both wars) who took it as their lot in life to remain single; often to care for their family.

Miss Lockwood was the senior lady though, taking the top class. It was her job to get us through the 11+ exams and on to grammar school, and spare us the "failure" of attending the Willows, the local secondary modern on Hibbert Lane only a five minute walk from home, and where most of our friends would go.

Mum was even more ambitious than our teachers. A proud and favourite mantra of hers was: "I've not always lived in a council house, you know." So it was important that we passed our 11+ to go to grammar school, and if that wish could be reinforced by having to pay for private tuition, so be it. My teacher was on Mount Drive and I can date the original Quatermass Experiment on television very precisely. My direct route home from Mrs Shaw's tutorials went past a house with a Quatermass-type plant-monster rustling in the garden. It scared the living daylights out of me. I would dare myself to pass by right in front of it. On less courageous days, I crossed to the other side of the road and if I was totally terrified I went home by a longer route.

And Now For Something Completely Different... ...living life to the full

Something paid off at least and I passed to go to Hyde Grammar School. Before that could happen, Mum spent hours on the phone trying to persuade the education officers to let me go to Stockport which was much more accessible (sorry, Marple's in Cheshire and Stockport is a separate authority) or New Mills (equally sorry, that's Derbyshire). Mrs Mills got herself quite a reputation. On one occasion, whoever took the call passed the phone on to a colleague and was heard to mouth: "It's the dragon of Hibbert Lane."

So started my new life at the age of eleven. Seven years of leaving home at 8 o'clock in the morning and returning at 5.30 p.m. - travelling by bus and train. Quite a change from the carefree years of playing along the canal towpath.

And Now For Something Completely Different… …living life to the full

Chapter 3

On to Grammar School

For some years I was a member of 1st Marple Cubs. My main memory of that period, apart from camping at Lyme Park and physical games such as British Bulldog, was the weekly queuing up at Jarvis's "chippie" for the obligatory "three pennerth" together with its free fishbits. That period of my life was completed by a trip to Luxembourg. Overseas travel in the early 1950s was a rarity and it was seen as a privilege to be able to spend time in an old army hut and sleeping on a straw palliasse. It was exhilarating and exhausting with non-stop exercise in the country's forests where our leaders scared the life out of us with stories of the local "gernomies"! I was the youngest member of the party so it probably hit me more than most. Mum told me that I slept solidly for three days on our return home.

For schooling, once a pass in the 11-plus was assured, Hyde Grammar School was our only option as both New Mills (Derbyshire) and Stockport schools were out of bounds to Cheshire children.

For seven years that meant the 8.11am bus from Stoke Lacey and the 8.26 train to Hyde Central (except briefly when I had a girlfriend who took the 8.16 and I was forced to make a special early effort). It was a long day as the return train didn't get back into Marple until 5pm. Then most of the time we ignored the bus home from the station in order to save the fare to fill ourselves up on Sheldon's penny buns. It was 5.30 one evening when a prefect accosted me in Marple and handed me a detention. The sin? I wasn't wearing my school cap. The injustice.

On the other hand there was a big gang of us, and going to and from school was a pleasure for the most part. Especially when the ice and snow came and the train was unable to get across the viaduct into Marple. We were expected to walk to Romiley (just a couple of miles) where it was waiting for us. Except on one memorable occasion when even that option wasn't available. We had to make it all the way to Hyde on foot. We were in no hurry naturally and it was just about "dinner time" when we straggled in, to be greeted naturally by several strokes of the cane. On the other hand if we had gone home instead, Mum would have given us the same welcome with the belt!

My "bestie" in the early days was the girl next door, Margaret Crook. Her Dad was "away" most of the time; Crook by name crook by nature as everybody said. But the the family was lovely. The two of us regularly walked up over the Ridge and through Disley Golf course before dropping down to High Lane for Sunday tea at her grannie's. Then Dad came home and they all moved to Australia

It seemed to us that our summer holidays, much of them spent down the road on Holland's farm, went on forever in never-ending sunshine; with adventures all the way down to (and beyond) the railway line at Rose Hill in fields and woodland now covered by housing. Daring each other to leap from high up in the barn, screaming "rats" to entice the farm dogs into the dairy so that we could play football in the yard (and of course retrieving the ball from the manure heap), delivering the milk - all part of the pleasures of a rural childhood. And damsons - there was an enormous tree by the yard, which is where I gained my lifelong love of that fruit.

I well remember playing cricket in the alley at Charlie Greenhalgh's place alongside their bakery and shop on Church Lane. The "square" can't have been more than two yards wide. It just didn't matter. But football was the big love. Apart from at school, there were no organised teams in those days. We had to set up our own and arrange matches with friends who had done the same thing. We met and practised on Compstall Rec, and played against teams in Bredbury and Hyde. To get there we had to walk or cycle. And if the opposition didn't turn up, it was just too bad. We played a game among ourselves and then walked five or six miles home.

I don't think we were ever in the house. Friendships ranged far and wide. We walked all over the place; Strines and Mellor were just like being next door. And of course the old quarry on Marple Ridge was a ready-made adventure playground.

Dad worked in all the neighbouring villages, at garages which did not have their own auto-electrician; but also from home. Days out were often aborted as an emergency job came in to get some family or other off to their holiday destination. They got to theirs, but we were left with another Sunday at home. Our summer holidays were always in North Wales in the early days -

around Abergele and Anglesey largely. Mrs Shaw's "big eats" in her guesthouse at Benllech were legendary. In later years, horizons were expanded to Devon; but to get there meant an overnight B&B stop. There were no motorways and Devon in a day was a journey too far.

I well remember a caravan holiday at Llanddulas. It rained all week. We had a bucket in the middle of the floor to catch the main leak. Then there were glasses and eggcups on the windowsills to catch the drips. A "high point" though was an incident with the portable toilet just outside. We woke up one morning to find that not only had it blown over but worse it had rolled down the railway embankment, and we had a pre-breakfast scramble to rescue it from the track before the "Welsh Dragon" tourist train trundled through to take it towards Llandudno!

Visits to Stockport Market were a weekly treat. The hourly bus from Glossop took us to the Rising Sun at Hazel Grove where we either caught a tram or the 92 North-Western bus into town (yes, it wasn't the famous 192 in those days). The Saturday market was a thronging mass of humanity with stall-holders shouting out their pitches all around you, fairground-like. Mum had a particular love of the "potman" on Castle Yard. Then we would go down into town. As children, we loved gazing down into the River Mersey as we crossed the small footbridge.

As a special treat, we would have a meal in the "posh" restaurant on the top floor of Stockport Co-op. In retrospect it must have been a pretty dowdy place by then, but we loved it.

And Now For Something Completely Different... ...living life to the full

As I moved into my teens, it became my responsibility to do the Saturday morning shopping at Marple Co-op (the Compstall Cooperative Society as it then was). I was addicted to the two hours of popular music of Saturday Club on the BBC Light Programme, leading to regular arguments over Mum's "Go now". The main shop was on Market Street. I loved ordering the butter and watching it being patted into shape and weighed out. *"And a pound of bacon please"*. The thickness setting on the cutter was always the main issue. The Co-op drapers was across the street and their butchery and fishmongers were around the corner on Stockport Road, opposite the Hollins Mill. I still remember my mum's "divi" number: 1885!

As we moved through school, it became necessary to earn a bit of extra pocket money. I had two main sources of income. First of all came my gardening customers, and then on Saturday afternoon, I did caddying at the golf club across the road from home. The normal "fee" was four shillings (20 pence), but the occasional generous golfer topped it up to five "bob". Then it was a race home to watch the Six-Five Special on TV - the first programme ever to be on between the end of children's programmes and adult fare in the evening. Not only that, but it fed my keen appetite for pop music, with Don Lang and the Frantic Five and Tommy Steele. Then it was off to Marple's Regent cinema, a Saturday night ritual.

Somehow, I moved on to ballroom dancing at the Beamsmoor School of Dancing in Marple. I loved it. And plenty of girls of course. Education always came second to pleasure. Even at school, debating, table

And Now For Something Completely Different... ...living life to the full

tennis and chess came first. At the time Hyde Grammar School had the second best chess team in Cheshire and we delighted in regularly defeating schools from all over the County. All that is except Calday Grange on the Wirral which twice stopped us at the ultimate hurdle, so that we could not represent Cheshire in the national championships in London.

In school uniform

Time to go into the 6th Form at Hyde. In the first week of that new life, I joined Marple Young Liberals. "I shan't be able to do much", I told them: "my education has to come first". Some hope, as I soon became Press Officer! Then there was football, dancing and dating. Teaching was to be the destination career, chosen above journalism and librarianship.

In the week that the "A' level results came out, I was in Denmark on a cycling holiday with other members of the Young Liberals and had to pick up the news from Copenhagen Post Office. They were always going to be disappointing; ability, but no application was the verdict. Certainly not good enough, it seemed, for my chosen course.

Chapter 4

And on from school

So... it was on to night-school for retakes and to take up a job in secretarial work at a Manchester Finance company with an office full of my "aunties". By good fortune, my English teacher at Hyde ("Uncle" Geoff Barnes) learned what had happened and was outraged. He was sure that my results were good enough - and so, after he had called on one of his contacts, at half-term I found myself enrolled at the City of Sheffield Teacher Training College studying History with subsidiary English. A whole new world had opened up. And with it even more leisure opportunities!

This was the beginning of great change in teacher training. For the first time, the course was to run for three years instead of two. In those days, a teaching degree did not exist and graduate teachers rarely did any professional training. The majority of us obtained a Certificate in Education. One benefit of the newly lengthened course, for us loafers, was that the planners had not really sorted out how to pack the extra year with coursework.

It was a happy time for a whole range of reasons. We had excellent teaching, especially in History where "Johnny" Johnson added to our experiences through the history society and by becoming patron of the chess team of which I was a very nervous captain. I was also captain of the table tennis "B" team and loved debating.

On top of that we started planning a drama review to put on before the whole establishment, students and staff, when the chap who was directing and was to have written a lot of the material selfishly got himself suspended from College. We met to decide what to do and somehow - I truly don't understand what happened - I was delegated to take over. Phew! A baptism by fire, but we didn't make fools of ourselves and even won some congratulations. Was this the starting point for later theatrical pleasures? Just maybe.

However, the most momentous change for me came from a member of our History class. Jeanette Partington was a slight, dark, quiet girl who seemed to shrink from attention. I have a strong feeling that her friends had something to do with bringing us together despite her inclination to remain unnoticed. Whatever! It certainly worked. Strangely, as things turned out, one of the things we had in common was that we were both seeking religious truths. Not only did we attend Christian meetings in College, but we visited a range of different churches and groups (some of them pretty extreme to put it mildly).

In the circumstances, it seems odd that during our final year, we both came to the same "big bang" conclusion - we were seeking for something that for us was (and still is) a fiction. That was a more momentous conclusion for Jeanette than for me, given her strict Methodist upbringing. I think therefore that the announcement of our engagement made to both families in Jeanette's tiny College room came as a bigger shock to the Partingtons than to the Millses. Their daughter engaged to a lad who had introduced her to the world of pubs. Oh dear!

And Now For Something Completely Different... ...living life to the full

Our generation was fortunate in being able to claim grants, and have our fees paid if our parents were on low income. Halls of Residence fees were covered and we also received a cash sum of £30 a term. While this enabled us to attend college, we still had to supplement it by working during the holidays.

While still at Hyde, I had worked as a postman at High Lane both during the summer holidays and during the Christmas rush period. Getting up at 4.30 every morning and then cycling two miles to the post office for a 5.30 start was a challenge. Such an early start was necessary because in those days, we not only delivered the mail, but had to do the sorting for our entire "walk". The Christmas Day delivery (oh yes, we *did!*) was a special and joyful experience, especially during a white Christmas, when some houses invited us in for a celebratory glass of sherry.

My first College summer job was with the Works Department at Marple Urban District Council (that was before the village was integrated into a greater Stockport). I started on a road gang - filling holes in the road and taking down old lamp posts, before moving onto the Marple baths. Apart from cleaning out the slipper baths and scrubbing the scum line in the pool, it was a lovely job supervising the bathers with the bonus of a free swim when we weren't busy. The most amazing thing in those Health and Safety free days was that they never asked for life saving qualifications.

Summer earning came to £35. Wow. So, with advice from my Dad, I was able to use what I had earned to buy my first car, a 1939 Standard 8 with the registration letters: BBU. The Yogi Bear cartoon was popular at the time and so *Boo-Boo Bear* it became! It trundled back and forth over the Snake Pass between Sheffield and home for the next two years.

My final summer vacation job was at Matlows sweet factory in New Mills, this time assisting the store-keeper in delivering all the ingredients to every department. What I saw going on on the chewing gum floor (quite literally) put me off that product for life. Every Friday we were able to buy things to take home at bargain prices. Mum loved their Chocolate Brazils, so that was a regular purchase. What I never had the heart to tell her was that I had seen the ladies in the top floor department putting the marks in the top of the wet chocolate with their fingers as it passed along the conveyor belt: lick, squiggle; lick, squiggle...

It was a good job that dad was an auto-electrician as he was kept on permanent callout keeping Boo-Boo on the road. But even he couldn't prevent Boo-Boo's final demise following a New Year's Eve dance in Cheadle. Malcolm and Alison (in a car considerably older than ours) towed us back to Stockport in the early hours of the 1st January. We abandoned it at a garage Dad had contacts with, and that was the last time we ever saw that old friend!

The Sheffield years were very happy ones, although they ended on a bitter note. We left College a few weeks before the end of the academic year, to make a start on our American adventure. I was due to receive a Distinction in English and only learned later that my tutor (who shall remain nameless) withdrew the

And Now For Something Completely Different... ...living life to the full

distinction because, he said, I couldn't be bothered to complete the course. How petty.

Another problem caused by our summer absence was in applying for our first teaching posts. It was a bit tricky because our return to England would not be until some three weeks after the start of the new school year. Perhaps not the ideal way to start our careers. Fortunately, Manchester saw things rather differently from some other local authorities. They told us that our summer activities were a positive, and were happy to employ both Jeanette and myself.

And so I started two happy years at St Anne's C of E Secondary Modern School. The "Annes" was truly tiny by post primary standards, only 120 pupils (boys and girls). As well as teaching History and English, I was in charge of the library and the school football teams. Sixty boys in four years (our pupils left school then when they were 15). There were not many decisions to make for the year teams with a total of 15 boys to choose from.

The small band of colleagues was very close, educationally and socially. We were out together every week; folk clubs, ten-pin bowling, the odd "pint", even short holidays. Then there were athletics meetings across the north west. We all participated in one way or another.

Going back to Marple meant getting back into politics. At first it was as the local Press Officer and representative on the Greater Manchester group. It was once again also very social, and we met regularly in each others' homes. "We are a very loose group," I once very memorably reported at a regional meeting, a revelation greeted by hoots of laughter.

And Now For Something Completely Different... ...living life to the full

Cheadle Constituency in those days was enormous (it has now been divided more manageably into two), but we had active groups in each of the four Urban Districts of which it was constituted. Somehow or other, I became constituency Chairman. One particularly memorable August was spent at a summer school at Girton College in Cambridge. I remember celebrating my birthday in my tiny bedroom with a crowd which included two MPs; not a bad haul, as I think we only had six at the time.

In my early political days, we worked with our prospective parliamentary candidate, Roger Cuss, a friendly and impressive local solicitor who managed to cut massively into the Tory majority. He stood down before the 1966 general election, and was replaced by Dr Michael Winstanley who was famous at the time for being the radio doctor (on the Home Service as it was then!) I spent many happy and productive hours with him and his wife, Joy, touring the constituency in his "battle bus".

Roger Cuss's previous record and the work we put into the campaign paid off. Michael Winstanley won the seat. Which led to the Young Liberals' biggest constituency event. Richard Wainwright had won the Colne Valley seat at the same election, so we organised a walk from Cheadle to Delph, about 30 miles. We were all very lively as we marched through the centre of Manchester, through Cheetham Hill, Prestwich and Shaw, as we loudly "megaphoned" our slogan: *"We're Going from Strength to Strength"*. We were less fresh and lively on our arrival at the end of the day.

And Now For Something Completely Different... ...living life to the full

The mid-60s was a key time for young people. Up until then the BBC had a monopoly on mass transmission of popular music - apart from Radio Luxembourg in the evenings. Even then listening to music through a crackling radio reception was far from ideal. The mid-1960s brought a big change to the music scene with the arrival of Radio Caroline and the Pop Pirate stations. We organised a day dedicated to the subject, culminating in a meeting starring a pop pirate DJ. It was truly politics for the young. Radio 1 was introduced soon after and popular music broadcasting was never the same again.

In parallel to all the politicking, we had decided on an early wedding, not much more than six months after we had started teaching. Given Jeanette's background, and if we wanted to continue a relationship with her parents, it would have to be a Chapel event. Meeting the Minister at his home at Irlams o' th' Height turned out to be an eye-opener; or at least the car journey was as he drove us back to Jeanette's home. He turned out to be an "Oh my God'er"; first as he jumped the traffic lights at the start of the East Lancs Road, and then after I queried whether he was going the right way to Tennyson Road: "Oh My God, I'm going to the wrong church!"

One of our wedding guests, Ruth Plate, flew in from Sweden on the eve of the event. I was driving over to collect Jeanette to head out to the airport to meet her when I had a slight collision with another car in Salford. Nothing serious; no injuries. But it did mean that BooBoo would be off the road for some time.

And so it was that Malcolm Allcard, my best man, spent a hectic morning on Saturday 10th April ringing round, trying to hire something that would take us on

And Now For Something Completely Different... ...living life to the full

April 10th 1965. With Malcolm and Jeanette's sister Kathy

our honeymoon. No joy - Good Friday in the 1960s and the car hire industry was not as developed as it is today. Nothing; not a thing. At the same time, Dad was phoning round garages to find something through his trade contacts.

"We have a Hillman Cob van," Church Lane Garage in Marple reported, "but you'll have to wait for it because it will need welding first." What is it they say about beggars and choosers? And so, instead of driving off in splendour after the reception at the Robin Hood in Clifton, we had to return to 85 Hibbert Lane to await the completion of the welding work. It was not what we had planned.

Our honeymoon destination? We had borrowed mum's cleaner's caravan for a week at Caernarvon. Luxury eh? But by the time our newly welded transport arrived, it was clear that we would not get there that evening. So we drove across Cheshire (no motorways in 1965) looking for a suitable B&B. No joy - and so we spent our first honeymoon night in a small street corner pub in Whitchurch. Celebrations were a pint in the small lounge bar. We awoke on our first morning of married life (no, we were woken) by the continuous chiming of church bells across the street from our accommodation.

Happily, we had already organised our first home and were able to drive back from our honeymoon caravan, straight to 18 Chadwell Road, Offerton. We were fortunate that mum and dad were able to let us have an interest-free loan to cover the deposit, but the house cost a grand total of £1,650 and we would need a £1,200 mortgage. "Sorry sir," they told us, "that is too much for your income." We were both working teachers, but the building society wouldn't take Jeanette's salary into consideration; not a penny of it. In the end, the sellers reduced the price by £100 and then lent us another £100 interest free. They were very keen to get their own move sorted out.

Then came the life changing advert in *The Observer* newspaper. Africa beckoned.

And Now For Something Completely Different... ...living life to the full

Chapter 5
A Minisink Summer

At the end of our student years in Sheffield, Jeanette and I decided to spend a summer in USA working as counsellors on summer camp. We applied to the Association for World Travel Exchange in New York and ended up with a group of young people from all over Europe who were to fly out from Schipol airport in Amsterdam. We had no idea where we would be placed; we would take what was given to us.

The journey itself was both interesting and complex. I was suffering from the after-effects of a vaccination and ended up with painfully swollen ankles which took away some of the pleasure of travel. But - I was not pregnant whatever the wags had to say.

The journey from Yorkshire to Schipol airport was by bus, underground, train, boat, train and bus! Students from various European countries gathered at a deserted airport that had closed down for the night. Well after our scheduled departure time, there was no sign of our charter plane; I asked at the only open desk. We don't know where it is, we were told. A fine start to our first ever flight. Eventually, we learned that it had landed at Gatwick by mistake. We had been told that we could not depart from Gatwick as the landing fees were too high.

Finally when we were able to take off; it was already towards the end of the night. We were hungry and thirsty with no local currency, but were provided with nothing to eat or drink. This was the era of propellor driven planes and ours could not cross the Atlantic in one hop. Our first stop was Shannon in Ireland. Then we moved on to Gander on Newfoundland. As we left the plane there, one of the cabin staff was heard to say to a colleague, "I'm glad that's over. I wasn't sure that we were going to make it." Hmm. If we thought that a transatlantic journey lasting for going on 24 hours was the longest we'd ever experience, we should soon learn something quite different. Because? Perhaps not surprisingly, Capitol Airways went "bust" during our summer stay; but that is another story for later.

After a pleasant but short stopover in New York, we were allocated our destinations. Jeanette was to go to a Jewish camp in upstate New York and I was allocated to Camp Minisink, belonging to the New York City Mission in Harlem whose town house was our starting point.

Camp Minisink

We were a group of white European students and one white American in a camp otherwise comprised entirely of US Negroes (as they called themselves in those days). The youngsters were from New York's district of Harlem, whilst the majority of the counsellors were from the southern States.

We were there bang in the middle of Civil Rights movement protests and we spent a lot of time singing freedom songs such as "We Shall Overcome" and listening to Joan Baez and Pete Seeger. Do you know, we never for a minute thought that we were doing anything out of the ordinary? It was all just normal. It was only later when we were on the road and meeting the general populace that we started to hear anti-black sentiments - to which we took great umbrage and with which we argued fiercely. We were frighteningly naïve youngsters who hadn't come across such bitter racial prejudice before. It bewildered us and angered us.

Those two months at Camp Minisink were extremely happy ones. We worked hard but had a ball at the same time. We were welcomed to camp by Gladys Thorne (Thornie), an imposing lady whom we soon found was feared, respected and loved (and not only by the children). She certainly knew how to run a tight ship, and to get the youngsters to enjoy themselves at the same time.

I was in charge of a hut of eight young boys in the Lakeside unit and I quickly learnt that trying to get them out of bed in the morning in the way I had spoken in England created laughter rather than obedience. It had to be "Hey you guys" in a strained, false, British tone; but it was accepted.

The knowledge of England and the English was non-existent among my young charges. So questions such as, "Gee Keith, you speak real good English. Where did you learn it?" were commonplace. On my day off I was asked if I was going home to see my mommy. Two of my colleagues were blessed with British prime ministerial names and there was more laughter as I shouted across the unit, "Come over here Winston, Churchill!"

The camp was run on native American lines and traditions and the big campfires with accompanying singing and dancing were something to really enjoy in the evenings. Of course after all that and all of our chants and shuffles, I had to have a head-dress to take back to Stockport.

We did hikes, lots of swimming, marshmallow roasts and overnight sleep-outs. "What do you want on your sandwiches, guys?" I asked before one expedition. Peanut butter and jelly (that is jam) was the reply. So we started making separate ones. "No, on the same sandwich", they yelled. That was another culture shock and one that I never fully came to terms with.

After one trek up to Crystal Lake, I experienced another shock. I was in the water with my eight boys when a ranger called me out and instructed me to get dressed. I was wearing my usual UK-normal swimming trunks, but they were not acceptable in the US. "We do not accept bikini wear for men or women", I was admonished. Very embarrassing.

On days off, we got the truck into the tri-states town of Port Jervis, a perfectly ordinary little place, but it made a pleasant break after a full week in camp and the valley road with river and railway alongside was very attractive. But the biggest new experience was to eat pizza. Would you believe it, we had never tasted it before? It had not reached England at that stage.

I wanted to be part of camp entertainment, and so I joined a staff dance troupe. The original idea had been to perform something from West Side Story, but that proved to be too ambitious. We ended up doing an African giraffe dance. We wore a kerchief and jeans rolled up to the knees; that was all. I must have looked the oddest of sights, contrasting my pale white body with a troupe of glossy black ones.

And Now For Something Completely Different... ...living life to the full

It was decided to put on a football match (soccer they call it), USA vs the Rest of the World. Hmm again! The American team was full of giant, fit young men, some of them on the verge of becoming professional sportsmen, albeit in different sports. The "Rest" was a mishmash of unfit, mainly European, enthusiasts. We understood the game; they were athletic. We beat them, would you believe? I clashed with a semi-professional American footballer and we were both carried off. Fortunately I was back to normal the next day; he was out for a fortnight. Result!

On one memorable evening, Thornie invited the international contingent to a campfire. We all had to sing something representative of our own country. But what made it so special was the presence of Irving "Lord" Burgie who wrote the "Jamaica Farewell", "The Seine" and a host of other songs for Harry Belafonte, and who performed for us after we had completed our amateur efforts. On the same evening we were honoured by the participation (not on his instrument though) of George Duvivier, the celebrated jazz double-bass player. What an evening that was.

What we truly did not appreciate was that we had arrived at the start of Freedom Summer, and we were there when Lyndon Johnson signed the Civil Rights Act in July, just months before Martin Luther King was awarded the Nobel Peace Prize. The racial undertones were for the most part lost on us. We were having a ball with some wonderful people; it was as simple as that. Some of the older teenagers on camp were naturally very angry young men and women. One evening (at a dance rehearsal) an 18-year-old was regaling the company on his hatred of the whites and what they were doing to his people. He was stopped and was tactfully reminded that he should tone down his remarks due to my presence. Initially he looked bewildered and then after a very short pause, he apologised with the words, "I forgot that you were white."

I do think that we became an integral part of their society and I was proud to acknowledge it. The pride was heightened when at the end of the season I was made an Honorary Tapawingo; the highest award they could give. I was massively proud of this and all these years later I still am. It brought the camping season to a wonderful conclusion.

The season was in fact divided into two halves with a break of camp in the middle. Apart from the European counsellors, all of the staff were black. The only exception was Pete who invited me to stay at his home on Long Island during the break, where we should be able to visit the World Fair that was taking place at the time, but more particularly to meet his father who he insisted was a true anglophile.

His pa, he told me, would "closet me in his den" and grill me about England. He did just that. "Where do you come from?" he wanted to know. "Manchester", I told him (the only possible reply in the U.S.). He knew Manchester very well and visited every year; so "Where in Manchester?" "Well not really there, but Stockport, a neighbouring town." Ah, it was Stockport where he went for his work. "Well, not really Stockport", I countered, "but a village nearby called Marple". Of course that is where he always stayed with a colleague named Elias. "And they have a daughter called Carole don't they",

And Now For Something Completely Different... ...living life to the full

I suggested? "I went to school with her!" It truly is a small world.

On the Road

At the end of the summer we returned to New York to prepare for our various hospitality tours. Some of our colleagues were crossing the country as far as California, but you had to pay extra for that, so we opted for a self-drive tour to New England, Canada and a round trip back to New York. It was to cost no extra!

There were to be 30 in our group, but not everybody was back from their camp by then, so half of us set off and the others were to join us later. Our first stop was Wilbraham, Massachusetts, from where we were able to visit Boston; though my most enduring memory is of proof-reading the Democrats' election leaflets. We were well looked after, but it was not a free lunch.

The next stop was Rutland, Vermont and a ride to the top of a ski run (though without the snow at that time of year). It was at the summit that the rest of the party (including Jeanette) made their rendezvous with us. Then came the bombshell; our "masters" in New York had decreed that I was to be tour leader. That meant of course that I had to drive; the first time that I had driven on the right and the first time in an automatic; and all with eight students and their baggage on board. On that first day, we missed a turning and I reversed in order to go back. There was a ditch on either side of us and long before I completed the operation, the passengers had all leapt out. Oh those of little faith.

The convoy of four cars then set off for Montreal in Canada. Once again we were well looked after with a city tour, a visit to the giant locks on the St Lawrence

And Now For Something Completely Different... ...living life to the full

At the Canada/USA border

seaway and an official lunch with the Mayor on Notre-Dame Island where you can now find the Formula One circuit, and a visit to the Caughnawaga "Indian" reserve. It was not all quite so exciting.

Naturally, I wanted to go out on the town with the rest of the "gang". We stayed with local people and my hostess had different ideas. She was an elderly single lady who had shared her house with a maid for many years. They may have lived together for a long time, but madam dined alone in the main room (though with me too on this occasion) while the "servant" ate in the kitchen. It was an enormous oval table, but the maid had to come along to pass things between us. Heaven forbid that I should make the effort.

That, however, was not the reason why I was not allowed to live it up with my friends. "Dr Finlay's Casebook" was on television that evening and she would not forgive herself if she did not permit me to watch and remind myself of home!

It was after Montreal that the ideal of our being on a hospitality tour started to come unstuck. It was hotels in several destinations from now on. Ottawa in the mist; a below par place at Niagara Falls; cabins at Clearwater Michigan where I had to address the town council in session; and Detroit where we managed a tour of the Ford Motors complex. I had to phone New York every day to find out where we would be staying the following night. Their organisation was appalling and often they still did not know until the very last minute. The number of calls increased by the day; for accommodation details, and increasingly to get permission to get one or other of the cars repaired. The tour and the vehicles had both begun to unravel. Everybody was still having a great time, but I could have done without the hassle which also caused me to miss out on one or two of the excursions.

Things got back on track in Chicago; though even here it was not really normal-normal. We stayed with a black doctor; yes, all 30 of us! He was supposed to find hosts for us, but he had a large house and just loved entertaining. We had a great time and everyone loved the atmosphere. The New York organisers were not amused however. They had not been consulted about these unusual arrangements.

We wandered down by the lake, shopped for folk music records on State Street, marvelled at the Marina Towers which had just been completed. In the evening a small group of us headed off to find one of the city's numerous jazz clubs. Jeanette and I ended the evening in a small place with a black (of course) pianist-singer called Claude Jones; cool and relaxing. We made requests and he met them. After closing time, we got to chatting and were invited to his apartment on the next day. That was an experience, a new world for us. It was enormous with panoramic views and a grand piano in the centre of the living room. After entertaining us, he took us on a city tour, particularly to see the deprived areas. We had seen nothing like it before; it was hard to take it in.

Before we left the city, one of the cars finally gave up the ghost. Although New York believed that it was repairable, it really wasn't. We had to abandon it in a parking lot and head off in a functioning replacement.

Next was Evansville, Indiana, and a Democrat picnic, then on to Cincinnatti. We then faced a 500 mile drive to Leesburg, Virginia. We set off in the morning with no idea of our destination (except for the town), and were not given a contact telephone number until late afternoon. It had already been a long day and arrival time was not expected to be until a couple of hours before midnight. Or so we thought. By now we were in the West Virginia mountains and had already been travelling for eight hours.

Of course it was while we were descending some particularly tortuous roads that the brakes decided that they had had enough and refused to work. All I could do was to put the car into low gear and crawl towards our destination at which we finally arrived in the early hours of the next morning. I drove around and deposited all of my passengers. Totally exhausted, I started to make my way back to my host family - on the wrong side of the road! Phew, I got away with that as there was nothing on the road at that hour.

The final part of our tour took in Washington DC and Baltimore before our return to New York. Although the role of tour leader took something away from some of the pleasures, it had still been an immensely enjoyable experience. And of course I was paid for the responsibility that had been thrust onto my shoulders. I do not think that anyone ever asked if I was happy to do the work. It was just taken for granted. So the £30 I earned was 'gratefully" received. That is right; £30 for a month's work!

All that remained before our return home was to strip the car of the coloured tape that had announced the countries of origin of the travellers and to do our final bits of tourism. The Rockettes and "Mary Poppins" at Radio City rounded it all off. Or so we thought!

Back Across The Atlantic

We had not realised that the adventure was not yet over. I mentioned earlier that Capitol airlines no longer existed to transport us back to Europe. AWTE chartered a plane from Icelandic Airways to do that job. It turned out to be an even more circuitous route than the outward journey. The first scheduled stop was Goose Bay, Labrador and then on for breakfast at Keflavik Military Airport on Iceland itself.

On our return to the gate, we were informed that the plane had developed an engine problem which would have to be repaired before we could leave. However free snacks were available. This was a pattern for this journey; every take-off and landing was accompanied by food and as good students everywhere, we were happy to take what was offered. By the time we got home, we were well and truly bloated.

The repairs were effected fairly quickly and off we flew towards our next destination, Copenhagen; we had a good proportion of Scandinavians on board. The captain pointed out the northern Scottish islands, but soon after we could not help but notice that one of our four engines was not working! Thus it was that we were diverted to Stavanger in Norway.

By the time that they decided that the engine could not be repaired that night, it was after dark and we were transported to a luxurious hotel where we dined and relaxed in more comfort than we had experienced all summer. To our delight the next morning when we drew back the curtains, we were overlooking the port. A magnificent sight. Breakfast consisted of a wonderful smorgasbord and it will be no surprise for anyone to read that we piled our plates up high. When we got back to our table we were then asked whether we wanted one or two eggs with our bacon! The gourmandising went on.

We then had the morning free to explore the town ready for a midday rendezvous at the airport where we learned that we were to be separated from the Scandinavians and were flown back to Schipol. We had been provided with enough money to return by bus and ship to Harwich. From there it would have been hitch-hiking to Stockport, but it was just as cheap to fly to Manchester. A flight was scheduled to depart before the afternoon was out and so we quickly booked our seats. We arrived at "Ringway" and telephoned my dad to beg a lift home. "I'll be there," he said. There was just one important request. He had to tell mum not to prepare any food for us. We had been stoking up almost non-stop for two days.

It seems impossible nowadays with modern air communications to understand that our flight to New York and back had involved our taking off and landing eight times.

And Now For Something Completely Different... ...living life to the full

Chapter 6

Zambia

When Charles and Kevin Ssentamu, our very good friends from City of Sheffield Teacher Training College, left to return home to Uganda in 1964, we told them that we would come and see them sometime. Well, you do say that, don't you? So when I saw advertisements for teachers to work in Africa, as a form of overseas aid, I immediately got in touch, filled in the application forms and was called for an interview at the Ministry of Overseas Development in Stag Place, London.

"We are coming to see you, Charles," we reported. But things weren't that simple. We couldn't pick where we went. It came as a total surprise to be interviewed by the Zambian education attaché and to be offered a contract in this newly-independent central African country. Ah well, we did not know one end of Africa from the other at that stage of our lives and we decided that it would be an adventure worth taking. Even my headmaster in Manchester, Frank Briggs, thought we were going to South Africa! Ignorance of the continent was pretty widespread.

And so... early in January 1967, both our families came together at Gatwick Airport to see us off on a British United Airways flight to Ndola. My first impression of Africa was to be the overpowering heat that met us on our brief stop-over at Nairobi; and that was at four o'clock in the morning.

After an overnight flight with no sleep, we joined a large group of similarly exhausted and bewildered newcomers in a large airport lounge. Was that green grasshopper safe for the children, everyone wondered as they surrounded the poor creature? Such was our ignorance. Then we boarded a rattling Central African Road Services (CARS) bus to the Hotel Victoria in town where we were booked into a room. We were exhausted and had no idea what was going to happen next or where or when we were going to be despatched, so Jeanette and I took it in turns to try to sleep. We were terrified that if we both dropped off, we would miss the next stage of our journey. Talk about innocents abroad.

We need not have worried. John McQueen, my new headmaster at Roan Antelope Secondary School, arrived, introduced himself and took us for our first bottle of Lion Lager at a local hotel and then drove us to Luanshya which was to be our home for the next three years. We were installed in the home of a colleague who was on leave in the UK and that evening went for dinner at the McQueens' home. It was not our most enjoyable evening despite the wonderful hospitality. We were dead on our feet and wanted nothing more than to "crash out" for an extended sleep. Our first African storm that night was unforgettable though, and despite our exhaustion, we sat on the verandah entranced by the majesty of the crashes and flashes and the rain pounding down on the metal roof of the house.

The next few days were all equally bewildering; drinks with our new colleagues at the Mine Club the following mid-day; interviewing servants (we had no clue on how to go about this terrifying task); getting to grips

And Now For Something Completely Different... ...living life to the full

with the school and its curriculum. This last matter was an enormous culture shock for me. After being responsible for teaching at the most basic of levels in a Manchester secondary modern school, I was plunged into Cambridge Overseas Certificate syllabus in English Language and Literature as well as in History. This was a newly independent country, so what was I teaching at 'O' level? British Empire and Commonwealth history of course!

In the end it proved to be a very satisfying life, and a revelation for a young couple whose background was northern English working class. We had so much leisure time with servants to take over all our daily household chores. School started at 07h.30 to avoid the worst of the day's heat, but then we were free from two o'clock each afternoon. It was like being transported back in time to the relaxed luxury of a Victorian middle-class existence.

Out of the classroom, life was made up of sports, followed by sundowners (what we later called aperitifs in France) at the Mine Club, the Rugby Club or the Cricket Club. There were parties every weekend when a group of us regularly gathered to belt out, mostly Irish, folk songs. It was a hard-working, hard-playing and, yes, hard-drinking society.

Luanshya was lovely, truly a garden town full of beautiful flowering trees. Our house was fitted out with basic furniture (and a never-ending supply of cockroaches), but apart from that we had nothing; our personal bits and pieces were presumably still at sea, and would arrive well, who knew when? We discovered that one advantage of living in a "mine house" was that we avoided paying for water or electricity; the miners had these charges deducted from their salaries and we worked for the government. Learning how to employ servants was a minefield; we were so naïve. There were people knocking on the door at all hours looking for work. Our first employee was James who was paid £7 a month + 10/- a week ration money. We found being called 'bwana' as difficult to get used to as the whole business of hiring and employing servants.

To buy new goods was impossible; things were frighteningly expensive and so we frequented the regular house sales, run by Dennis Figov, where people who were leaving the country auctioned off their stuff. The sooner we could acquire our own things, the sooner we should be able to return everything that people had lent us.

In these circumstances, we needed Jeanette to find a job. I was on contract of course, but that option was not available to married women in those days; they had to find work where they could once in Zambia and they received local pay which was not great. We were lucky when we heard that a miner's wife wanted to give up her job. Which is why a friend, Margaret Moss, took her down to "chat up" the Mother Superior at the Convent Primary School where she was duly appointed.

Our biggest acquisition was the purchase of a car; for the first time in our lives we could have a new one instead of the old "bangers" that had always needed my dad to keep them on the road! That was only possible because the government would provide a car loan. We opted for

And Now For Something Completely Different... ...living life to the full

a Toyota Corona from Pearts garage in Luanshya. By delivery time though, prices had risen, and we were able to opt for a "horizon blue" station wagon version which had held its price at £840. The car loan was £550 added to a top-up advance from Barclays Bank. It was still not enough so, "Mum, please send us another £50 from our meagre UK savings." At least Kevin had managed to sell our old car in England and that was £10 that came in handy in the circumstances.

Teaching was a joy in that our students were desperate for knowledge. To have any discipline problems, you had to be really incompetent (and we did come across the odd teacher who was!). At that time the boys had to pass an examination at the end of their second year in secondary school if they were to be allowed to stay on for two more years to study for their "O" levels at the end of year four. The variety of work was exhilarating with classes at all four levels in all three subjects. It seemed so worthwhile. In addition, I took on responsibility for the library (just as I had at "the Anne's" in Manchester) and took great pleasure in reorganising it thoroughly.

John McQueen was an idiosyncratic head teacher and chose his Heads of Department purely by watching them perform in the classroom. I served under two excellent Heads of Department, Joan Estcort at English and Margaret Gregg in charge of History, and when they left I was given the choice of taking over either of their posts. My appointment in Zambia had primarily been for History, my main subject, but I chose to lead the English staff as there was an allowance for this but none for History. An extra £60 a year was not to be sniffed at.

And Now For Something Completely Different... ...living life to the full

In their turn, Roan Heads of Department watched their staff in action so they could give advice on how to develop their teaching techniques Then, mark this, we had to give "master classes" for our staff. Actually this system proved to work very well.

Our everyday life was disrupted during our first year in Zambia by the late-arrival of our packing case and with it those bits and pieces that were intended to personalise our African home and its standard-issue furniture. When it did arrive, there were, of course, breakages and we had to go through the protracted and, it seemed, fruitless claims procedure. Successive letters, each one becoming more irate, to London, Manchester and Lusaka elicited no responses whatsoever.

Finally, an article in the "Observer" brought things to a head. It asked readers if they had ever tried to get money out of an insurance company and concluded that it was easier to rob banks. I cut it out and wrote yet another letter, expressing my agreement with the conclusions, signed myself "Bank Robber" and once more posted it off to London with the clipping attached. We were only claiming £30, but that was not an inconsiderable amount in our lives at that time. A week later, normally mail took a week each way, I was teaching when there was a knock on my classroom door. "Leave the lesson, you have an important visitor," I was told. It was an agent from the insurance company. What had I said? He had received the biggest rocket of his life. After I had confirmed that he deserved it, he took out a cheque book. How much do we owe you? It was only after he had gone that I realised that I had been too honest. I could have asked for anything.

Before the middle of 1967, we realised that our life was going to change quite radically. Jeanette was expecting our first child. Everybody was pleased for us, even though it did not come as any real surprise to anybody. Almost every young wife was in the same "club". Pregnancy was known as "Luanshya disease".

With a child on the way, we were going to need a two-bedroom house and so late in August we moved from 94B (Buntungwa) Avenue into 37Y (Yarrow) Avenue. Our new house was truly filthy and the furniture was terrible. We were moving from mine accommodation to a government house. It was so bad that we had no hesitation in refusing to sign that it was in good condition as requested. Dickson, who was our diminutive but delightful garden servant by this time, worked hard to clean the place from top to bottom, and government workers did their bit with redecoration and repairs. Eventually it started to feel like a real home, but Dickson subsequently fell ill with stiff and aching limbs. I'm not surprised after all of his sterling efforts.

The Effects of UDI

Our three years in Zambia probably fell at the worst possible time. Ian Smith's Unilateral Declaration of Independence (UDI) in Rhodesia on November 11th 1965 not only affected that country's existence, but ours too. The supply of oil products coming from the south was cut off by economic sanctions. Early in 1967 our monthly petrol allowance was 10 gallons and the only way to eke this out was by car sharing to get to school. That was a pleasant enough experience, but very limiting.

Things got even worse during the rainy seasons. Most of our petrol supplies came along the untarred, dirt road from Dar-es-Salaam. That was bad enough during dry weather when the journey could take some 13 hours, but during the "rains', transit time rose to 20 hours. Even worse, there was usually an accident a day with tankers skewed into ditches along the whole length of the road. It is no surprise that it was known as the "Hell Run".

The other crippling effect was on the export of Zambia's precious copper, the product which kept the country's infrastructure operating. The only alternative transport option was by air! Petrol started to arrive in pot-bellied Lockheed C-130 Hercules transport planes and when they left they were loaded down with copper wire bars. It seemed to observers that they would never get off the ground at Ndola airport. Amazingly they always did.

The fuel crisis affected one major decision in our lives. The Luanshya Mine Hospital was only round the corner from where we lived; very convenient for Jeanette's ante-natal appointments. We nevertheless decided to register with Kitwe Hospital, 60 kms away. Madness? You would think so, but the attraction was that we got an extra petrol allowance for the regular visits.

Jeanette was due to finish work in mid-October but, because the convent school was short-staffed, she agreed to continue on a week-to-week basis. It was even more noble (and profitable) given that she was still recovering from a twisted ankle and was also due to take her driving test at the end of the month. It was an established "fact" that everybody failed on the first attempt, and passed the second time around; more

And Now For Something Completely Different... ...living life to the full

revenue for the coffers that way. However, after a final practice session on reversing around the football pitch penalty area and in and out of the goals at Roan, she managed to squeeze back into the driving seat and did the unthinkable; she passed first time. We suspect that the examiner was afraid that he would have to deliver the baby if she had to go back a few weeks later.

At the final ante-natal appointment, the doctor said that, because of earlier high blood pressure, he would have to induce if Jeanette had not gone into labour by the following week. This was quite common in Zambia at the time and we always wondered whether it was anything to do with altitude (we were on a plateau at over 4,000 feet). Anyway this was unnecessary as Nicholas William arrived late in the evening of 8th December 1967 and, as Jeanette wrote home, "fit and healthy with no bits missing".

I had come into the hospital that evening, but the sister sent me home as an imminent birth was highly unlikely - she said! So it was that I was having a beer with Peter Cox in Luanshya's BUFFS Club when the news came through that I was a dad. We were in the perfect place for an immediate celebration, which is why I had to stay at Peter and Joy's overnight to recover and be ready to drive to Kitwe the next morning. Visiting meant an anxious daily 120 km round trip. There were problems with anaemia, and a blood transfusion was necessary, but we finally took Nicholas home on 15th December.

A New Responsibility
The start of 1968 brought a touch of madness to my professional life. I had been teaching for just over three

years and I found myself having a responsibility placed on my shoulders without the experience to back it up. John McQueen, our headmaster, had been suffering serious back problems, culminating in his being rushed into Ndola hospital. Jerry Sexton was Deputy Head, but he was away on leave. Wally Myburgh took overall charge of the school with me as his assistant, if for no other reason than that we were there and available. At the time I was acting Head of History.

My task now was to organise the first year intake. The first appointment was a meeting with the primary school heads and followed by welcoming 37 children the next morning at 8 a.m. On the same day I was scheduled to have a meeting with the Chief Education Officer from Ndola. I also had to greet the new teachers arriving from England, while Wally took charge of timetabling.

If that was not enough, I had to sort out the History syllabuses for the whole school. I had previously been asked to prepare them for two of the four years but with John out of the picture, I had to take his share on board as well. With the Headmaster in hospital and his Head of Department on leave in New Zealand it also fell to yours truly as the department's remaining "senior" member to take responsibility for the exam classes. Worse was to follow.

The petrol situation suddenly worsened. We were down to five gallons and, even with a small essential user's allowance, we quickly learned that the best way to get into school was by bicycle. I had not done so much cycling since I had been a schoolboy myself. By the middle of that month, and with everything more or less under control, we were ready to let our hair down a little. Jeanette and I plus Peter and Joy Cox decided to go down to a "do" at the Rugby Club, dancing to the "Bees Knees". We dolled ourselves up, the girls in their best dresses, Peter and I in collars and ties; and what did we find when we arrived? It was a "tramps" fancy dress do. Perhaps people thought that was our way of slumming!

By the end of January, the fuel crisis had reached a new low. In the midst of the rainy season, the Hell Run carrying the precious fuel from Dar-es-Salaam closed completely while diversions were cut at the worst points. Tractors were roped in to drag stricken tankers out of the ditches. Luanshya's pumps were bone dry and by the time they were restocked in February the petrol coupons were invalid. If you had not used them by the time the worst of the crisis bit, you lost even that small allowance. One secondary school had to close down entirely as a result. It was worse than the time of U.D.I. when the monthly allowance had been four gallons. The bright spot on the horizon was that we were promised that the new pipeline would be completed before the next rains. Our fuel problems did pay off in one small way when I wrote an article on the Hell Run which was published on the leader page of the Manchester Evening News, and for which I received the princely sum of 5 guineas.

Petrol Rationing and Holidays

It has remained a great disappointment that during our three years in Zambia, we were able to see so very little of the country. There were just the occasional visits to Ndola, ante-natal visits to Kitwe and other trips to assorted Copperbelt towns for theatrical performances or sport. Unfortunately, spontaneous days out were rarely possible. It was very sad that our Zambia years had such limitations, and so the ability to holiday outside Zambia became very important. We were issued with enough petrol vouchers to get us to one of the country's borders and then back home again when we returned to the country. Inevitably that took us south to Zimbabwe, or Rhodesia as it then was.

The first time that we got on the road was with the Coxes in the April after our arrival in the country. We piled into their car and headed off for Kariba with its famous lake and dam. The road to Lusaka was excellent and gave us a rosy feeling for motor travel. Later we had our first experience of strip roads where vehicles approaching each other have to share the tar and put one wheel onto the unpaved section. You soon learned that the game was to play chicken. Could you keep all four wheels on the road, forcing your "opponent" through the dust or mud, depending on the season. Single strips were the easy ones. Far more difficult to navigate were those where there was only enough tar for the wheels, and what was in between could be extremely nasty.

Our arrival at Leisure Bay Motel at Siavonga took away all the stress from the journey and we could relax on the shores of the lake. Wonderful, even if the diet did tend to be a bit limited; Kariba bream three times a day. To be fair, the chefs did ring the changes magnificently; they must have had the widest range of bream recipes of any hotel in the world.

Then someone had the bright idea of crossing the dam and heading on to Salisbury (now Harare). All that way

- and what did we do when we got there? We went to a night club to watch drag queens and a stripper known as "Fluffles the tassel twirler"! I made the mistake of sending a card to my mum telling her of our change of plans and panic set in back in Marple. She was convinced that we were going to have our heads chopped off. A prepaid reply telegram was waiting for us back at Box 9 in Luanshya when we got home. All it said was, "Is all well?"

The next trip was due in September; but oh no, it was not! Luanshya was supposed to be malaria free, so when my temperature rose, the doctor treated me for 'flu. Needless to say, things did not get better and of course by the time my temperature reached 103°, the government medical man had been transferred out of town and had not been replaced. A private doctor gave the correct diagnosis, but the tablets he prescribed would not stay down, and although the subsequent injection did work, our holiday had gone, along with the symptoms. The reaction from James was: " Bwana, you are thin; too much." I am afraid that state soon got reversed ... and more.

Joe and Anita Hennessey had just arrived from Belfast and were staying with us by then. We had missed our September holiday, but not to worry, we could get away at Christmas. Oh no, we could not. I had forgotten about the arrival of Nicholas William!

Money concerns refused to go away though and a third mouth to feed merely accentuated these problems. Once again, not to worry, we thought. We were due a tax refund, and by the standards of the time, a considerable one. Unfortunately the months passed and no refund arrived. The only solution was to travel to Lusaka to sort things out. We sought and received a special petrol allowance and our bank manager agreed to back an overdraft to meet our accommodation costs. We headed into the tax office full of confidence that very soon we should be leaving with an inflow of funds.

Life is never that easy though, is it? "You have already received the refund cheque", we were told, "and you have cashed it." "Oh no we have not; or we would not be here." Time passed; investigations were made. Finally it transpired that there had been another Keith Mills in Zambia. That he was a volunteer who had never paid tax, and that he had left the country with our money cut no ice. Finally we got to the chief inspector of taxes, a bluff and intransigent Yorkshireman. They could not make a refund on the spot because that could only be done under exceptional circumstances. We detailed everything, but no, it was not considered exceptional. Things were beginning to get louder and louder in the corridor. Still no, no. no! Until, right on cue, Nick started to bawl very loudly indeed. That proved to be the necessary exceptional circumstance and we left with our cheque!

Mum had decided by this time that she was not going to miss the opportunity to fly out to see her first grandson. It was truly no small decision. Until then she had never crossed any sea (unless you can count holidays on Anglesey!). It was quite an undertaking. Transport arrangements were put in the capable hands of "uncle" Horace Edwards who was manager at Thomas Cook's in Manchester. Of course he could not get it right for mum. The flight that he arranged from Manchester to Heathrow was cutting things far too fine (she reasoned) and an earlier one had to be booked. Even after the transfer to Gatwick, she was far too early for the British Caledonian VC10 to Ndola. Her nervous panicking did not go unseen and she was ushered into a lounge and plied with brandy. The final solution was for her to be upgraded into first class where she was kept company by an airline employee who was off to a friend's wedding in Nairobi; his sole companion before mum's arrival was a barrel of English beer destined to make sure that the festivities went off with a swing.

Mum's First Grandson

She certainly had a great time. She loved the flying even though her first experience of Zambia was a negative one - she deemed Ndola airport to be a dump. Whether it was or not, it was the scene on many occasions for "pouring" drunken departees onto their flights as they high-tailed it back to London on BUA VC 10s. Her time in Luanshya was one great social whirl. An event of great family note was mum's introduction to Lion

Lager on a hot day at the Kitwe Agricultural Show. That was a life changing experience for her!

We soon headed south to experience the wonderful Victoria Falls known locally as Mosi-O-Tunya, the smoke that thunders, and then onto the Wankie (Hwange) Game Park, the first real experience of wild life for all of us. What we had not anticipated was that this was going to be a particularly cold southern African winter and, given that we were staying in unheated budget accommodation, mum was finding it particularly difficult. By the time we got to the national monument at Great Zimbabwe, she was sleeping fully dressed under a coat in the non-insulated rondavels where we were lodging.

During our tour, we bumped into some fellow Zambian teachers who, in the circumstances, had better remain nameless. Over dinner one night, we were told that they too would like their parents to visit them in Zambia; it would be a great experience. Unfortunately, it would not be possible because they would have to take them on a holiday (just like ours) and that would put too many miles on the "clock" of their car and lower its resale value far too much to be acceptable. It was hard to credit; their parents were missing the holiday of a lifetime for the sake of a couple of thousand miles!

We carried on to Umtali (Mutare) and stayed in the beautifully situated Christmas Pass Hotel. There were no problems with feeling the cold here as we relaxed with our drinks in front of a roaring log fire. The return journey home included another stop in Harare, then back to Zambia via Chinhoyi (Sinoia) and the Blue Jays

And Now For Something Completely Different... ...living life to the full

Hotel at Karoi with its legendary breakfasts, surpassing even the mixed grills available for the evening meal!

If it had been cold on our travels, we were horrified on our return to Luanshya. The line of trees on the entry into our beautiful garden town were sporting blackened leaves, there were sad-looking banana trees all over the town. That the frosts had hit so far north in Africa was something of a nasty surprise. Even more surprising was the report in Britain's Daily Telegraph that there had been snow in Zambia. If that had been so, we should have been approaching a new ice age I suspect. There had been hoar frost and a rural meteorologist, who had never seen such a thing, reported it as snow.

Life at Roan Antelope continued to be an enjoyable challenge, social life continued apace, sport remained central to life, and theatre had become a new passion both at adult and school levels. I have recorded these last two activities elsewhere,

For the Christmas break, we had decided to go down to the coast to Beira in Mozambique. Ronnie and Eleanor Hollywood were with us until Umtali (Mutare), but we travelled on alone to stay at the Estoril on the shores of the Indian Ocean. We had never experienced such humid heat in our lives; not a pleasant experience. As soon as you came out of the shower, you needed a shower. Not being people who enjoyed spending hours on the beach and finding the town centre rather uninteresting, we decided to return to Rhodesia (Zimbabwe) for the New Year celebrations.

By the time that we got home, John McQueen had left Roan and we had a new head teacher, Mr Ike Thoka.

Things were bound to change with a totally different person in charge and a whole new atmosphere in the school. We had already decided that we would move on from Zambia in August 1969 and this change confirmed that we had been right to make the decision.

Before that though we had the Easter holiday to plan. We took driving long distances for granted by now. As we did not have the petrol to explore Zambia, we had to go beyond the borders. This time it was going to be Swaziland and Durban a round trip of over 3,000 miles - if we didn't add any detours during our break!

All went well on our outward journey through Zambia and Zimbabwe. It was not until we reached the South African customs post at Beit Bridge that there was a hiccup in our plans. The clearly racist officer took an instant dislike to our Zambian registration plate and that white folk were living in the "black north". We needed an address in the Republic if we were to be allowed in. We were on a book-a-hotel as we went holiday and the telephone number of a friend was not deemed suitable. Two hours later, with Nick getting fractious and night coming on, he conceded that an address in Swaziland would be acceptable; we were visiting friends of a South African colleague. We had offered this objectionable man this option 120 minutes earlier, but he ignored it at the time for no other reason than to cause us trouble.

What he did not know, and nor did we at the time, was that he had done us an enormous favour. We had planned to be 100 miles down the road that evening but, as we crossed the Limpopo, night was fast approaching and we decided to stop at the first hotel that we found on the left in Messina, just nine miles away. That decision - on the left - was crucial as we ignored the one that we passed on the right.

Accommodation for a couple plus small child please? No problem sir. Please sign in.

It was while we were writing in the register that we both did a double-take. Two fellow students from our days in Sheffield were approaching reception. They had already been to their rooms and were heading for the bar. Not surprisingly, my first reaction was to suggest that it would be great to share a few beers together and "chew over" the old times. "You ain't seen nothing yet," was the response. "Look in the bar". And sitting there was another couple; more student companions from those "old days".

There are coincidences, and there are coincidences! Four people meeting up at the same hotel in Africa was one thing. Three couples doing that took them to an entirely different level. Especially as none of us knew that any of the others were even on the same continent. And, oh yes, all of us had driven down from Zambia. If my memory serves me right, we sank more than the anticipated few beers that night.

Swaziland does not take long to explore! You can get from one end of the country to the other in little over two hours, so in the afternoon we set off to explore the country. We were entranced by what we saw and did not notice how time had passed or, more importantly, where we were and this was not a country where there were road signs. Time to go back to basics we thought; the sun sets in the west so ..... this must be the way back to

Manzini and our hotel. It was not until we reached the same cross-roads for the third time that we had to rethink our tactics. So much for being the great explorers.

Our principal destination on this holiday was Durban. Apart from the beaches, our main memory of this town would have been the wonderful scents and sights in the Indian spice market. I say "would have" because yet another coincidence struck us. We were walking close to the shore when who came up to us but Raj. He had been a very good friend, but had recently left Luanshya to return to his homeland. It was an amazing thing to happen and this is where the effects of Apartheid really struck home. We could not sit on a bench together; we could not go to a café or bar and we could not visit his home because we had not applied in advance for a permit to do so. It was great to see him, but it could have been so much more. And that was the last time that we ever saw him.

Our return home was to be via a short stay in Johannesburg. In the hills just before the municipality of Estcourt, we were held up interminably behind a small car. Very frustrating. Finally, just before the town, there was a straight bit of road. We went for it, passed him and slowed as we entered the built-up area. Then we spotted our friend speeding up to overtake. Suddenly the police siren started up and we were gestured to pull over.

The cap went on and another example of South African police intransigence and hostility hit us. We had touched a solid white line as we passed him. We would have to go before the magistrate and pay a fine before we would be allowed to go on. That was bad enough, but it was Friday evening and we would have to spend the weekend in a police cell until the court reopened on Monday morning. It was not a pleasant thirty minutes as we tried to reason with him. Were we rescued by 18-month-old Nick waking and deciding that it was dinner-time? We shall never know why this officious man finally decided to let us go back to the "black north".

Ready to Leave

We were into our final term in Luanshya, after which we were due to leave at the end of August. Before that Nick was due to have a new brother or sister, we had all the packing up to do, and I was organising my farewell schools' drama festival at Roan.

Number two child was running late. On the morning of 8th August, Jeanette had the car and I got a lift to work. Off she drove for ante-natal where the following conversation took place. "You are leaving in three weeks, aren't you? I had better induce. Can you come in now?" First of all though she had to take Nick to the creche and send a message to school to tell me to pick up the car from the hospital car park. Fine, except that before the end of classes, Rogan had been born.

All that remained was the farewell party. We had booked the cricket club for the event. We had been members there for some time and when at the previous AGM a group of us complained about an exorbitant rise in membership fees for non-playing members, they responded by electing us as Vice-Presidents. In that way, they got even more out of us in donations! So it was that very shortly after leaving the Roan hospital,

Jeanette and a very pregnant Eleanor Hollywood sat in our living room peeling and cutting potatoes for a hotpot for 70 people. We went out in a great big stew!

We were ready for the next stage of the big adventure.

Chapter 7
Rogan's First Safari

The big "off," our final departure from Zambia, was on 28th August with a (under) two-year-old and Rogan at just 3 weeks. A journey by road, rail and sea which was going to mean he was 2 months old by the time we got back to England.

We drove from Luanshya to Lusaka. We had a buyer for our car in the capital. What we would have done if he had failed to turn up with the money, I shudder to think. Anyway, it all went well, and I have a vivid memory of walking through the city streets with several hundred pounds in Zambian Kwachas in my pocket, terrified of being waylaid.

Two days later we caught the tourist bus to Livingstone and Victoria Falls where we were to spend our last few days in the country. We had booked for a few days' rest in a small but comfortable rondavel (we had stayed there with Mum the year before), close to an outdoor café with a sign on the tree "Beware of Crocodiles" and within hearing distance of the Falls, Mosi-o-tunya, the "smoke that thunders". We did a lot of walking; it was probably going to be our last chance to see the area. We still have the solid wooden elephant table that we bought for mum and dad (it is sitting in our living room). I can certainly testify to its weight, especially after wearily carrying it for what seemed like miles in very high temperatures.

On the final morning we took a taxi to Livingstone station. We did not dare miss the train, especially as our packing case was scheduled to be on it, and I had opted to clear it through customs all the way back to England. The journey over the Falls was a memorable one as the train was flanked by armed soldiers protecting the bridge. Remember that this was in the period following Ian Smith's declaration of Rhodesian independence (UDI) and guerrilla activity to overthrow him was beginning to be a real threat.

We were told, and it is a lovely story - as well as adding piquancy to our departure - that this was the last passenger train that ever crossed the Falls before sanctions and warfare took a firmer grip. We have to believe it, don't we?

Train Ride to Cape Town

The train ride to Cape Town took four days. We were comfortable enough in our sleeper and the restaurant served decent food and South African wines at a very reasonable price. The first problem came when we had to change trains at Bulawayo. We got ourselves installed in our new carriage before I got off to walk along to check that our packing case had been transferred from the Zambia train. But there was less time available than we had realised, and I was still on the platform when it

And Now For Something Completely Different... ...living life to the full

began to move off. Fortunately, slowly! So I was able to jump into the guards van in time - and there was our baggage; no need to have worried at all. But of course Jeanette had no idea where I was, and she was imagining that she was on her way to South Africa all alone - with two small children.

The other major problem was keeping Nick occupied. It's not a baby that is a problem in these circumstances, but keeping a two-year-old occupied in the confines of a train's carriage for several days took some imagination. Which is how we came to be showing him my Zambian driving licence which boasted a photo. "Ooh daddy," said Nick, immediately tossing it out of the window. So ... somewhere in the Kalahari is a 55-year-old document. A little piece of history lost in the sands.

Apart from the two things above, our main memories of the journey are of the social side; travellers' friendships in the bar, food and wine in the restaurant car. This was the start of the process of an appalling weight increase. You cannot travel for five weeks with so little exercise. There are two other memories: one was the stop at Gaberone in Botswana where the station was thronged with people selling food and crafts and haggling for goods through the carriage window. The other was seeing the great craters of the diamond mines in the earth at Kimberley, South Africa. So much ugliness caused to create things of beauty.

Following our arrival at Cape Town station, there was another hurdle to surmount. We had arranged to hire a car for our week's stay in town. Of course they wanted to see my driving licence first. And you know what had

And Now For Something Completely Different... ...living life to the full

happened to that. So what about my British one? Well, that was in the packing case which by now had been taken into the bonded warehouse ready for onward transmission to UK!

The company officials listened in amused silence. But then, "All right, we believe you. Nobody could make up such a story." I just cannot imagine that any car hire company would nowadays be so understanding and flexible in its approach. But it did give us the freedom to explore the Cape area at will.

Our hotel was by the sea; not four star luxury but comfortable enough, and with the bonus that they had a live band playing every night. So while the two little ones slumbered under the watchful care of the staff, we danced the evenings away. Most particularly, and every night, to "Spinning Wheel", the "Blood, Sweat and Tears" hit. And by day, we explored the region, one day driving down through flower-covered countryside, with monkeys climbing over the bonnet, until we reached the Cape of Good Hope. The view from Table Mountain at night with a beautiful fairyland of lights spread out beneath us across the city was something very special.

The weekly departure of the mail boat from Cape Town was still treated as an event to be celebrated at that time. We all stood out on the deck of the Pendennis Castle as streamers were thrown and, when we steamed out of the harbour, all the boats in the vicinity hooted their farewell. It was quite an experience, especially with the backdrop of Table Mountain.

I think that one of the reasons why we have never been on a cruise comes from that twelve day voyage from

And Now For Something Completely Different... ...living life to the full

Cape Town to Southampton. Nick and Rogan spent most of the time in the ship's crèche while we ate and drank; in addition to the normal three generous meals a day, there was also morning coffee and afternoon tea. And when it is all at government expense ..... !

Every morning they opened the barriers that allowed us commoners into the first class section so that we could take our daily constitutional round and round the deck. But it was nowhere near enough to keep the flab at bay. Otherwise it was the standard round of entertainment, bridge playing, dances and fancy dress (I remember us as caveman and his woman). Of course, there was too the traditional and formalised pool-side ceremony for crossing the equator, complete with water fun and King Neptune.

The only two stops were at the Canaries and Madeira. On the former, there was time for a bus tour of Grand Canaria and a cabaret at a local club. We were sitting near the back, but for some reason a dancer picked on me and dragged me along, pulling out my shirt, tying it around my waist and hissing, "Dance", as she pulled me onto the stage. We seemed to have a lot more friends the next day! Very amused ones.

We were not able to leave the ship at Madeira. It was too large to enter the harbour so new passengers were ferried out by launch and those departing were taken off, and a fleet of small boats surrounded us, selling all sorts of crafts. Goods were hauled up to us on ropes; we haggled, and the money was sent back down in a pouch.

We crossed the Bay of Biscay on a blissfully calm sea (we had been prepared for the worst), and sailed into

Southampton on the morning of 30th September; a beautifully sunny autumn morning. Though one South African woman standing next to us on the deck did not appreciate it as she said to her friend (in very upper-crust tones), "Of course my dear, it never gets properly light in England."

On the quay watching for us were both pairs of grandparents doing lots of waving and pointing. But first we had to get through customs and immigration. And for this, we had made another mistake. After three years in Africa, we were very afraid of being cold back in English weather. So we had dressed ourselves in layers of sweaters and coats. Oh dear! As we joined all the queues to go through the formalities, we were all but reduced to grease-spots.

Our hire car was ready for us; grandmas and grandpas were introduced and after the children had been cooed at, we all retired to a hostelry in Winchester for lunch before making our several ways back to Stockport and Swinton. Rogan's first "safari" was over.

Chapter 8
Uganda: The Koboko Years

We arrived at the old Entebbe Airport on the morning of 15th May 1970. A new one was later constructed during the Amin era and financed by Yugoslavia. This ramshackle old airport that we flew into became famous as the site of the raid on Entebbe by the Israelis when they freed the hostages who had been taken there after their plane had been hijacked.

After the drive to Kampala, we were checked into the Imperial Hotel, a comfortable but old-fashioned colonial place. Our early impression was of a cosmopolitan city where the three main races (African, European and Asian) were comfortable in each others' company in the streets, bars and restaurants of the capital city. It was a refreshing change from Zambia and, although there were obviously all sorts of under-currents that new arrivals could not see, it augured well for our stay in the country and gave no hint of the expulsions that were to cause so much havoc only two years later.

The other joyful event was the arrival of our old friend Charles Ssentamu whom we had not seen for six years since his departure from Sheffield at the end of our College courses. In addition to it being wonderful to see him, he was very useful in helping us to find a second-hand cot for Rogan (who was still only nine months old).

After a short stay in the capital, we headed for Koboko, beyond Arua in West Nile, and we were advised to

And Now For Something Completely Different... ...living life to the full

make an early start. Just how important this was only became apparent later in the day. The government car was loaded with all our baggage and the cot strapped onto the roof. Charles was there to see us off on our first Ugandan safari.

By the end of the day, we were somewhat less enthusiastic than we had been at the start. We headed north into the unknown. There were many miles of undistinguished bushland until the Karuma Falls livened things up. The Falls, and their resident crocodiles, were later to become notorious in the Amin régime killings. But for the moment, the setting was innocent and attractive.

It was not long before we turned off the tar onto our first experience of murrum (red earth) roads. Our route to the Nile bridge at Pakwach took us through the Murchison Falls National Park. As we approached the river, we saw the wonderful great herds of elephant that roamed freely in the area. It later became the family joke that the whole place was a total "irrelephance" which was trotted out each time we took that route.

Pakwach itself was a small, dusty place with no attraction at all apart from the bridge which joins the West Nile District to the rest of Uganda. The countryside became much more attractive as we climbed up towards the local capital, Arua. But by now it was getting late and it was not only the children who were finding the day long and trying.

By the time that we reached Arua, the pitch black of the African night had closed in and we were exhausted. But at least we were there! Or so we thought. We kept expecting to pull into St Charles Lwanga College any minute, but the road went on and on and we got more and more depressed. Where had they sent us to? Only later did we learn that it was the most distant state secondary school from the capital. Our previous privileged middle-class existence on Zambia's Copperbelt had not prepared us for this.

In fact it was a good hour after Arua that we finally drove through the township of Koboko and onto the school campus to be met by two of our teacher neighbours and the Italian priest headmaster, Father Francis Cifaldi. "Cif" was a large man, not tall but showing evidence of an enjoyment of the good things in life. Wearing as always his cassock, he greeted us in his distinctive and enthusiastic version of English.

First Impressions
The following morning, refreshed by a good night's sleep, we were able to inspect our new surroundings which were to be home for the next two years. Our first house was a two-bedroomed, semi-detached bungalow. Our immediate neighbours, Jeremy & Ann, were the art teachers at the school. The front verandah was enclosed with mosquito netting, but no glass.

Our electricity supply came from the school generator which was switched on when darkness fell and turned off again at 10 o'clock. So we had lighting for three hours, although the power was not sufficient to run any household appliances. We had the impression that its main purpose was to allow the students to study after dark, rather than for the greater convenience of the teaching staff. Amazingly, we had previously received a letter from the Ministry of Education in Kampala informing us that the school had "immense electricity"; in local pronunciation that adjective signified "mains". How wrong they were. Turn on any appliance and everybody's lights went out. Not "immense" in any sense of the word.

The contrast between here and our previous urban experience of Africa could not have been greater. We were clearly going to have to learn to be more flexible in our approach to life. The village at Koboko had little to offer us in the form of facilities. There were a few basic dukas, tin-roofed bars and a football pitch next to the village hall.

Most difficult for Jeanette, and she certainly found our new way of life tough in the early days, were simple things like the inability to buy what we had always considered to be the essentials of life; most particularly fresh bread. Arua was an hour away on that murrum road which became very difficult during the "rains". At first she thought that a weekly visit to the shops there, and in particular the Asian supermarket run by the Stankiya brothers, would help to make life easier. In reality, it would sometimes be several weeks in a row before we managed to get into town. The solution of course was home-made bread, but it took a while to get used to even this small change.

You would hardly expect that a visit to a little town like Arua would be anything special, but it brought variety to our lives. It was where we bought our little portable radio so that I could set my alarm to wake me up at three o'clock in the morning to listen to World Cup football matches from Mexico. I would hold it pressed to my ear in an attempt to get past the hisses and crackles of short wave broadcasts. It was at the Arua golf club that I played the only full round of golf of my life - and I won the competition. This had nothing to do with my ability; they drew the winning score out of a hat.

On the way home from town, we invariably stopped off at Ombaci School where the Verona Fathers and Brothers had a little shop where we could make purchases not available elsewhere. Being good Catholics, they produced some very good liqueurs!

A matter that we had to deal with early on was the employment of servants. We had got used to this reality of expatriate life in Africa during our years in Zambia. Now we started all over again. Jeanette was going to teach at the school so we needed to find someone to look after the children. Father Cifaldi introduced us to Rose (a good Catholic girl!) whom he put forward for this role. We took his advice and employed her immediately. In time, we would also take on a house servant and a gardener.

The school, the boys and our colleagues
The St Charles Lwanga College (Koboko Secondary School) took in boys for the four years leading up to the Cambridge Overseas Certificate. With an Italian priest Headmaster, Ugandan teachers from various parts of the country and British, Irish and American staff, it was a truly cosmopolitan environment, especially for the pupils, most of whom had never ventured beyond Arua.

To say that the headmaster was eccentric is to put it mildly. "Cif" had arrived in the village in the late 1940s before there was a trading centre and certainly before there was the church that he came to oversee. His first job was to have someone build him a bed.

We never knew whether his idiosyncratic use of the English language came from Italian or local Kakwa influences. But we did know that when one of the boys came to us and asked, "We hear people say ..... is that right?" they were talking about the "big man's" use of English. And a big man he truly was in character and stature. I have never met any other headmaster who arrived at staff meetings with crates of beer. His favourite "tipple" on these occasions was often a beer and coca cola shandy! Indeed!

His football field was of bigger dimensions than FIFA permitted for even the most important international matches. "It will make the boys run," he explained. I was not popular when he caught me bringing it down to an acceptable size.

But my favourite memory of Cif was his selection process for boys entering Senior 1 (the first year of secondary school). First of all, students had to have passed the primary school leaving exam (PLE) at a good level to have any hope of getting into a state senior school. Secondly, the new entrants had a wide range of ages. There were no birth certificates at that time and to a great extent we had to take on trust the ages assigned to them by primary school headmasters. Added to that was the fact that they kept on repeating the exam until they reached the required standard.

The registration procedure on the first day of term arrived, and there were invariably more candidates than places available. The walkway outside the administrative block was almost a metre higher than the central quad. The school uniform included grey shorts. We were not supposed to admit pupils above the age of 16 years; it could be a tricky judgement. But Cif's method of discovering overage candidates was nothing if not innovative. He walked along inspecting knees. We soon got used to the shout, "Knees too old. Off!" And off they had to go.

Of course this still meant that there were 11-year-olds and 16-year-olds in the same class and it goes without saying that it was the bigger ones who always got into the school football team. Not very fair on the little ones, so Cif created a special team for the smaller boys - it was known as the Giants.

Early Days
One thing that we had to get used to quickly was the school routine. Lessons started at half-past seven in the morning and we taught for two periods before it was time for breakfast for which the staff hurried off home. Classes finished at 1 o'clock. The afternoon was set aside for sport and private study. There were also evening study periods when one of us had to be on duty to supervise. On Saturdays there were inter-school sports events and in the evening there was sometimes a film projected onto the outside wall of one of the classes. The Catholic Father, Brothers and Sisters certainly did not understand the double entendre of the Carry On films. Just good, clean, knock-about fun.

Our diet was fairly limited. As already noted, bread became a luxury. We grew as many vegetables as possible in our gardens and twice a week a cow was slaughtered at the local market to provide the boys with meat. We appreciated fillet steak; fortunately the locals did not and we got our little luxury at a knock-down price. The only other meat was an occasional chicken, also from the Koboko market. Of course it arrived alive and was kept alive until we were ready to consume it. The bonus was that, if we were lucky, it provided us with eggs in the meantime.

Student strikes were not unknown in Uganda in those days and I remember one particularly amusing event when the boys downed pens in support of their vegetarian friends who, they complained, were not getting enough chicken in their diet. The word "meat" in their language meant "beef". If you did not eat beef, you were a vegetarian.

During that first term, for transport to Arua, to other schools and to local events, we were totally reliant on our colleagues. They were invariably very helpful, but we wanted to be independent, and so when the August holidays arrived, the priority was to get down to Kampala and seek out our own vehicle.

On this occasion we were able to spend time with Charles and Kevin Ssentamu and their children; more friends for Nick and Rogan. Charles had by this time become Principal of Busuubizi Teacher Training College near Mityana and we were to spend several short breaks there over the next few years. Charles of course knew the ropes during our used car search on our limited budget.

We ended up with a VW Kombi which over the next few years doubled as transport and purveyor of all manner of goods from cases of beer to sacks of chicken food; as well as accommodation on our holidays around the

And Now For Something Completely Different... ...living life to the full

Back with Charles and Kevin

country when we failed to find a hotel. If night caught us with nowhere to stay, we could always head to the nearest government secondary school where a member of staff would invariably let us park and sleep in their garden (three of us on the seats and Rogan over the engine at the back). Our hosts' bathrooms were always available for the niceties of life.

Loaded up with provisions for the new term, we headed back north in our newly acquired vehicle. It ran well and the fuel gauge made it clear that we had plenty of petrol to get us to Pakwach and the Nile Bridge where we could fill up. How were we to know that the gauge was faulty? Part way through the game park, we passed a pride of lions; the signal for Nick to insist that he had to get out and attend to the needs of nature!

Shortly after this, we shuddered to a halt, out of petrol and still a good way from any habitation. It was a deserted almost traffic-free spot, so we were filled with delight when we espied a petrol tanker heading towards us. Sorry, sir, said the driver, I am carrying diesel! We were lucky though with the second passing vehicle. He had a full can in his boot and we were soon on our way. That was another basic lesson quickly learned. Never let the fuel level get too low and always have a spare supply of fuel available.

Our second term commenced and we got back into the routine. We made our own entertainment for the most part with visits to Arua and other schools (often with the football team) among the highlights. We would walk up to the top of Koboko Hill with its view over the school and surrounding countryside and hiked to the top of Mount Wati which locally was believed to be the home of the spirits of the ancestors (bodies had to be buried with heads towards this centre of legend and faith).

Ann & Jeremy adopted a hammerkop which was unable to fly because of a damaged wing. During the day, it lived by the water tank at the back of the house and even came into the kitchen if it believed there were "goodies" to be safely liberated. Every evening, our hammer-headed companion walked down to the shed to be safely locked away for the night. It stayed happily until the day came when it was able to fly off again. We regularly saw these birds overhead and wondered if "ours" had come back to inspect its erstwhile home.

Nick too had a "pet". We had been invited to Rose's home to meet the parents of our children's ayah. It goes without saying that they were extremely poor, but the hospitality was as generous as it always is in Uganda. We left with a chicken - a gift for Nick. Like the hammerkop, it retired to the safety of the shed every evening, until one night some wild creature managed to get in and leave us with nothing but a pile of feathers.

It was with great excitement that we were soon able to move into new and much more spacious accommodation. The houses had been built with finance from the World Bank. In that setting, they were luxurious but less than sensible planning had been employed. They were equipped with immersion heaters and plenty of electrical sockets and lights. But apart from those three hours a night, there was no electricity. So we still used the old paraffin fridge and heated the children's bath water over a wood fire in the garden.

The two years spent at Koboko were probably more satisfying for me than for Jeanette, partly because the men had more freedom to get out and about than the women. Most of it was simply going down to the village bars with the "boys". It was a pretty basic experience, but there were unusual exceptions. Like the bar running out of beer and Jeremy going home to collect a crate to sell to the bar owner, who then sold it back to us at a good profit.

On one occasion, when I thought that we were heading back at the end of the evening, I was surprised when some young women got in the Landrover which then turned in the opposite direction from home. We ended up in the middle of the bush at a duluka; a dusk till dawn dance under the stars with only drums for accompaniment. Sometimes we drove up the road towards Sudan and a village called Keri. Here the road was the border between Uganda and Congo (Zaire as it was at that time). We turned the car round and parked on the left (Uganda) and crossed the road (border) to drink in the Congolese bars where the beer came in litre bottles and was so much cheaper than "back home". If the authorities had turned up, we would have had to run across the road into Uganda, which was why the car was where it was.

The Start of the Amin Years

Much changed in January 1971 when Idi Amin Dada assumed power while the previous President Apollo Milton Obote was out of the country at a Commonwealth summit in Singapore. At first there were celebrations, especially in our part of the country. Amin was born in Koboko, very close to where we were living. In fact, the then army commander was a regular visitor to the school where Cif bullied him and treated him like a naughty child to be ordered around. On one occasion, he demanded an aerial photo of the school for Geography lessons; and duly received it.

In Amin's early days, there was not a great deal of change to our lives apart from the dusk to dawn curfew that was in place. That did not stop us going out in the Landrover (eerily without lights) and spending evenings in bars with their shutters closed.

But for most of the time, it was the same old routine. Our boys thrived; there were lots of children to play with and although there was a different language spoken in almost every household around us, all the children seemed to understand each other. Apart from English, there were three languages in our house. Mary (Rose's sister who had replaced her) spoke Kakwa, James (who did the cleaning and cooking) spoke Lugbara. So when together, they often communicated in Swahili. I really believe that Nick and Rogan thought that everybody had their own language. They were able to tell us all sorts of things in tongues that meant nothing to us at all. On one notable occasion, we asked what they had said, and they told us: "That's our language!" We shall never know how that might have developed had we stayed there longer.

Naturally, many aspects of life were alien to natives of urban, northern England. Nick answered the door one day and came running in, "Daddy, Daddy; it's the smuggler". Remember that we were living on the border. For the most part his goods were pretty innocuous; plastic sandals, beer and for a real treat an occasional live guinea fowl that he had trapped. They went into our chicken run and were kept for a feast on special occasions.

Our isolation made such special occasions seem even more so. There were "dos" with staff from other schools (often through sporting events) and big one-off events like an early morning visit to the white rhino sanctuary. On our short ramble, we came across 21 of them of all ages. That is an occasion I shall never forget, made even more poignant and heart-breaking by the subsequent hostilities that led to their extinction in this particular area. There are other enduring memories like the overpowering scent of the eucalyptus trees and the piercing sound of the cicadas. On a different level, and memorable for very different reasons, was an inter-county Cup Final that I was invited to referee. Not surprising really. I was one of only two qualified officials in the area; and the other chap was responsible for the organisation of the competitions. So this very inexperienced official was regularly called upon to oversee some of the more important matches in the region. This included one where Idi Amin was present, and he insisted on meeting Mr Referee, before he made his speech to encourage his fellow Kakwa people. Clearly I lived to tell the tale.

A village experience of a much less pleasant kind came one St Patrick's Day. Why only two of us were available on that particular night, I have no idea. But with John's Irish background there had to be a celebration of some kind so the two of us headed off to a village bar. We were joined by a party of policemen from Arua who had been touring the local police posts distributing wages. It was clear that they had had a glass or two at each stop; but Koboko was the last one before they returned to home base.

All was very pleasant; lots of chat and sharing of experiences. Until...

It was now past eleven o'clock and I mentioned that by this time in England all the pubs would be closed; "how stupid", I commented. Now that word is much more derogatory there than in Europe, and it was overheard. "You are calling us stupid; you are calling us dogs." The atmosphere had turned sour very quickly.

It became very threatening. They marched us in; they marched us out. They ordered us into their Landrover which was the last thing we were going to do if we could help it. By now the murders and disappearances that were more and more going to be the trademark of the Amin years were becoming known. They were going to take us to the army; we would never see our families again, they threatened. We knew the village; they were very drunk. A run through the huts, shambas and chicken runs of Koboko was not a pleasant prospect in the pitch black of an African night but it was a more attractive proposition than getting into that vehicle.

In the end, this was not necessary, they got fed up with the whole business and left us in peace. It had been a frightening experience but we were safe, The next day, the two of us drove into Arua to make an official complaint at the police station. We were listened to sympathetically and promises were made. I very much doubt whether any disciplinary action was taken however. Threats are definitely colour-blind. I had now been threatened with death by a white policeman in Rhodesia (Zimbabwe) and a black group in Uganda.

Health and Allied Problems
On the health side, I suffered from some terrible night-time bouts of asthma (this was before inhalers, and tablets didn't do the trick) and a couple of attacks of malaria. Nobody told me about the affects of chloroquine poisoning, and after the first treatment, I ended up crawling up the garden on my hands and knees to get to bed. But they were as nothing to when Jeanette succumbed to hepatitis. The nearest Grade 1 hospital was two hundred murrum miles away in Gulu. Brother Luigi drove her there and she later reported that his dirt-road driving was terrifying, possibly worse than the illness itself. Clearly he put his trust in his faith.

But if Jeanette was safely ensconced in hospital for the next four weeks, I was in for an interesting month. The first weekend a shock absorber came off the Kombi just as I was leaving the school. I had to refit it twice before reaching Arua, where I found a garage that "fixed" it and promised me that all would be well and I could carry on with my journey. Not a chance, and after two more lots of running repairs, I took the offending item off altogether. The trouble was that I was running late by now and on the approach to the Nile Bridge at Pakwach, a real African storm could be seen blowing up. And once it arrived that would be the end of daylight.

That was not an insupportable problem in itself, but then I discovered that I had a battery problem. I could either put the headlights on, or the windscreen wipers. But not both. So for another hour, I battled along very difficult roads with the lights so that I could be seen, but driving with my head out of the window so that I could see and with the roads turning increasingly to mud. When I finally reached the main street at Gulu, the poor old thing (not me) shuddered to a halt. It was left there overnight while I begged a lift to a secondary school outside town where I could seek a bed.

Now... the following weekend. Everything had been fixed. All was bound to go well, wasn't it? So the decision was made to take the boys to see their mum. This time we only got a few miles beyond Arua when our long-suffering old Kombi shuddered to another halt. We were lucky to find someone to tow us back to town. Remember this was well before the era of mobile phones; in fact phones of any kind in many places.

I trailed the boys into the golf club with the forlorn request for a bed for the three of us. On the third weekend we actually got to Gulu without incident and mother and sons were reunited for the weekend.

Our hosts in Gulu, Syl & Sonia O'Byrne, proposed a bit of relaxation with Sunday lunch at the Acholi Inn. Except that Syl was unwell. So it was down to Sonia and me to escort our two boys and their three girls, all five of whom were of similar ages. As we walked into the restaurant, a very loud American voice filled the room with, "Gee honey look at those poor people". No, not at all; the two of us had not produced five children in about three years!

Mum and Dad's Visit and the End of our Contract
Mum had really got the taste for travel after her visit to Zambia. This time though Dad was able to come along too. The cheapest flight was to Nairobi and we drove there to pick them up. They loved our stay at the Ainsworth Hotel and our drive back through the Rift Valley via Naivasha and Nakuru, up into the Kenyan highlands and on to Kampala. We stopped off at Murchison Falls on the way home. It is such a beautiful spot that they could not help but love it. Except for the flying golf balls! These were some kind of beetle that flung themselves at you in the lodge corridors and terrified the life out of Mum.

Nor was she impressed by Koboko. The rustic life of north-west Uganda was far from her idea of pleasure.

I think though that all this was well compensated for by the rail journey they took between Kampala and Nairobi. on their way home. We had made the same journey ourselves and it really is a spectacular ride.

Just to finish off our first two years in Uganda. It had become clear that the lack of a degree was a hindrance to what I wanted to achieve (I had just a Certificate in Education). After looking at the possibilities, a

University of London external course seemed to be the best option. I decided on Honours English. But first I would need to add to my GCEs. So all of the time that I was coaching the Koboko boys for their 'O' level English Literature, I was going home in the evening to study the same subject at the next grade! I also had to study Latin at ordinary level, a necessity at that time for an Honours degree.

Towards the end of our time at Koboko, it was time for my exams which had to be taken in Kampala. They were not a problem even though I had to negotiate a few days off from teaching duties to become a candidate myself. In the end, it was all worthwhile, and I was ready to go on to the next stage; studying for a degree by correspondence. But that dear reader, as they say, is for another time.

We left Koboko in May, just two years after our arrival and spent a few relaxing days at the Apollo Hotel (later to become the International and then the Sheraton). Coincidences continued to crop up in our lives. As we got into the hotel lift, who should be standing there, but Dick Davies, our deputy headmaster from Luanshya in Zambia. We hadn't even known he was in Uganda! And that story had still further to run. Stay attentive please.

Chapter 9

Uganda: Life Under Amin

My main memory of our leave during the summer of 1972 was how very cold it seemed when we went on holiday to Cornwall, with the children paddling in the sea wearing anoraks. It was a long way from swimming in Lake Victoria. But Jeanette and I did manage to get a lot of walking done during the long summer evenings, leaving the boys with their Grandma and Granddad so that we could finish off our exertions by reminding ourselves of the joys of real ale in pubs always strategically situated at the end of each ramble.

Things had clearly deteriorated in Amin's Uganda during our absence; mind you the British press has a great knack of making things seem even more frightening from a distance than they are on the spot. However, things were to become more serious on 4th August 1972 when Amin (acting on one of his regular messages from God) announced that every Asian living in Uganda, whatever was on his or her passport, had just 90 days to leave the country.

What the consequences would be, for the men, women and children concerned, and for the country itself, were impossible to predict, but it was clearly going to be a time of enormous upheaval. On a personal level, it left us on the horns of a dilemma. We were due to fly back to Entebbe a week after the announcement. What should we do? Cut our losses and stay in England losing everything we possessed back in East Africa or take the risk and head into another adventure?

So we flew back. The initial impression could not have been more pleasant. We were installed in Lake Victoria Hotel while arrangements were made for our return to teaching. Nick and Rogan could not have been happier, gamboling on the lawns in great delight. They certainly thought that they were "home".

Before our departure from Uganda, we had negotiated a transfer for our second tour so that Nick could attend an English-language primary school, and Jeanette had managed to find a post at the same school. Lake Victoria Primary School in Entebbe was just a few miles down the road from where we were to live. At that stage, it was still a very colonial-type institution with a British headmaster of military bearing; a very formal establishment.

I had secured a post at St Mary's College, Kisubi. It was a very prestigious place and the oldest Roman Catholic secondary school in the country. Brother Anthony Kyemwa was its first African Headmaster, but many of the staff were still British expatriates. That was to change radically during our two-year stay.

The British High Commission instructed all UK passport holders to keep their bags packed in case it became necessary to get us out of the country at short notice. Before too long, we took the unilateral decision to unpack them - and we never did receive any different advice.

But if it was a slightly worrying time for us, it was a terrible experience for those being expelled. Men, women and children who had lived in the country all their lives, many of them holding Ugandan citizenship, had to leave with nothing at all. Everything that they had worked so hard for had to be left behind. Often they were robbed of what they were carrying as they travelled to the airport.

They were desperate to sell what they had, and as they could take very little out of the country they needed the payment to be made abroad. What a risk! Not only were they getting rid of their precious possessions at rock-bottom prices, but there was no guarantee that they would receive their money. They just had to take people on trust. Our old Kombi was becoming more and more of a liability so we took the decision to buy a small Fiat from a departing Indian family. We had a bargain, but at least we knew that they had something waiting for them when they arrived in England to start their new lives.

I must say that throughout this time, we never felt particularly in danger. If a European went missing, it was world news and even for this regime that was an important consideration. Of course it did happen from time to time; but it was the African Ugandans who were most at risk. Another black face went missing; that was hardly international news. It was a terrible time for them. By the time we left, we hardly knew a family that had not lost someone. We marvelled sometimes at people managing to continue their ordinary lives without falling apart.

We all got on with it. And I must say that, despite everything, we passed two more very enjoyable years in Uganda. In the daily routine, it was sometimes hard for us to see that we were in the midst of a whirlwind.

And Now For Something Completely Different... ...living life to the full

Talk about the chalk and cheese! Life at the arid, remote Koboko was very different from the green and pleasant Kisubi on the banks of Lake Victoria. The school even had its own private beach at Nabinonya. Most afternoons after school had finished, we were able go down there to swim, picnic or just relax. Here Paradise and Hell existed side by side.

With my 'A' levels behind me, I now started studying for an external English degree from the University of London. It was sometimes difficult to know what level of essay was expected as a correspondence student, but it was still a real pleasure to study works of literature that were in themselves so enjoyable. I was again Head of English which was a new challenge for me in such a prestigious school. As at St Charles Lwanga College, I was teaching 'O' level language and literature, but this time I was at least an extra step ahead of my students. As a non-graduate, I was not allowed to teach 6th form lessons at St Mary's College, although from time to time, I was called upon to take "master classes" to demonstrate to my young, recently-qualified local colleagues just how it should be done. A bizarre situation indeed.

One of the literature texts I had to teach was Wole Soyinka's "Kongi's Harvest", the story of a corrupt African dictator. A sensitive issue in itself, but when my class contained the sons of two of Idi Amin's Ministers, I was extra-careful about my interpretation of the text. Although I had by now spent several years in Africa, I was the new boy and had not yet tuned in to the various currents that were flowing underground everywhere in the country.

I must have been more obviously tactful than I realised. One Sunday morning, a delegation of students from this particular class came knocking at our door. They were served soda and biscuits and we discussed everything from the weather to football. The real purpose of their visit was not raised until ..... "Sir," said their spokesman, "we have noticed that you are very careful about what you say when we discuss 'Kongi's Harvest'. We understand why, but with our class it is unnecessary. Please say what you want to say." Such maturity on such young shoulders. I took them at their word. That class was a delight to teach.

For the most part the waters of learning flowed smoothly. An exception was caused by one of Idi Amin's many messages from God. Early one morning, he had been told that schools must close that day and the children should have an extra day's holiday. Schools had no option but to do as they were told. From time to time, we spotted a government helicopter overhead. We were being checked on.

On a totally different level was the occasion when our school band decided, in concert with the girls at Gayaza High School, to play at a dance at the girls' school. What they did not do was get the agreement of either our headmaster or their headmistress. Inevitably they were caught out. I do not know what punishment was doled out to the girls, but our boys were immediately suspended from school, told to go home and inform their parents of what had happened and not return until the next term. Apart from the shame, I dread to think what extra punishments their fathers would inflict. Little did we know that two of the band members did not vacate the school as instructed. Three weeks later they were found in the dormitories. They had not missed any of their education as their friends had relayed the lessons to them and they had done every scrap of homework that had been set. Dedication and self-preservation rolled into one.

A Third Parental Visit

Despite the misgivings of their friends, Mum and Dad decided to come out for another African holiday. By this time, travel was more difficult to organise as the number of flights coming into Uganda had been cut enormously following the political crisis. Eventually we decided on a flight to Nairobi and then an EAA transfer to Entebbe. The transfer time was not great, but we believed that it should be possible as long as the flight from London was not too late. Of course it was very much behind schedule and it looked very much as though they would have to stay in Nairobi overnight.

However as the plane taxied to a stop at Embakasi Airport, the doors opened, a man entered and called, "Mr & Mrs Mills. Follow me please." Mum and Dad followed him under the plane to the hold and were asked to find their baggage which was then loaded onto a carrier with the passengers and transported directly to their link flight which had been held up especially for them. What service!

Meanwhile, we were waiting at Entebbe, not knowing whether they would be on the flight at all. By the time the plane arrived and most of the passengers had disembarked we had decided that they must have missed it, but then they appeared at the top of the steps, the last passengers to disembark. "Look, Grandma and Granddad," we pointed out to the boys. A nearby immigration officer heard and said that they could go through to meet them, and the two of them raced across the tarmac. Can you imagine that happening nowadays?

In the event, we were able to give them a wonderful holiday; around Kampala and Entebbe and taking a trip to western Uganda, staying at Mbarara and on to Lake Bunyonyi - the lake of a thousand birds. We stayed in a school dormitory in Kabale and dined out at the White Horse Inn - Dad's favourite. We then drove up to stay in the lodge at Mweya in the Queen Elizabeth National Park and on to the Mountains of the Moon Hotel at Fort Portal.

Another Family visit

The difficulty? By this time, we were in our tiny Fiat, a squash in itself for four adults and two children, but when it started to overheat during the trip, we had to carry extra water wherever we went. A frustrating problem that an Mbarara garage did nothing to sort out.

Dad looked on in disbelief. It was not until we had got back home that a place close to Kisubi fitted a second radiator. The problem was never completely solved, but it did make life easier.

Extra pleasures for Mum and Dad's holiday were times spent with Charles and Kevin Ssentamu (Charles had stayed with them in Marple in 1963) and with John and Edith Ssemakula who had become friends when I supervised their teaching practice at Kisubi. Until the day she died, mum kept the necklace they bought for her from a seller across the road from the Speke Hotel. It was a precious memory.

A Memorable Holiday in Kenya
Our major holiday abroad was a memorable one near Mombasa in Kenya on the Indian Ocean. On this occasion our biggest problem was money, though not in the usual sense. The Ugandan shilling had by now no international worth. We had reserved our sea shore accommodation in advance in UK currency, but we would still need spending money. The plan was to meet up with a local businessman and sort things out, shall we say, somewhat informally.

We took the train to Nairobi - that journey itself, through the beautiful Kenyan highlands, made it a very special break. We then took the overnight sleeper, due in Mombasa the next midday. We had arranged to be picked up at the station. Unfortunately, we awoke the next morning to discover that we were stationery and still just outside Nairobi. So on our very overdue arrival in Mombasa, there was no one to meet us, we had no transport and no usable money. It was a long 6-mile

And Now For Something Completely Different... ...living life to the full

walk out to our beach resort - especially in the coastal heat and with two small boys. Fortunately, we didn't have to go the whole way on foot as we were picked up by a generous driver, and we got a lift back the next morning to sort out our financial embarrassment.

After that though, we loved such an idyllic spot; bathing in the clear blue seas, taking dhows out to the coral reef and walking along the beach to a hotel that specialised in fresh seafood. As we had hired a car, we were able to get up the coast as far as Malindi, as well as exploring Mombasa itself.

An Ever-Changing Situation
Our next-door neighbour in Kisubi was the legendary JC Kiwanuka, Uganda's first graduate teacher who had also briefly been Minister of Education, and who at this time was Deputy Head and in charge of the Maths department. He and Brother Anthony oversaw a largely expatriate, white staff, but this changed as, slowly at first, and then with increasing rapidity, Europeans felt that they were not comfortable under the Amin régime and left. By the end, we felt a bit like pioneers in reverse!

However, our relationship with the family next door was cordial and relaxed and Florah, their daughter, was a regular playmate of our children. On the other hand, we had brought our dog Simba with us from Koboko and she was not an ideal neighbour. She guarded the joint pathway and Florah's Mum often had to seek help to get past and into her own house.

We were privileged to be insulated from the worst of the horrors and we learned to use our common sense as to where we should not be at sensitive times. Jeanette had more difficulties than I did in this respect, as she had to drive into Entebbe every day with a car full of children. There was the daily problem of the army road block at the entrance to the municipality. It was a common occurrence for everyone to have to get out of the vehicle for checks, and for the children to have their lunch boxes opened and examined. Jeanette's hair was very black in those days and in one frightening incident a barely literate soldier accused her of being an Asian woman. If indeed Asian, she should have left the country some time before. In his view, the clincher was that she was carrying her British passport. Q.E.D.

It does not sound like it, but we spent two very happy years at Kisubi. The teaching was challenging and satisfying. Social life continued to be a real pleasure both with Jeanette's colleagues at the Lake Victoria Primary School and with mine at St Mary's College, although the racial balance at both places changed radically. By the time we finally left, the majority of our friends were Ugandan rather than expatriates. In a bizarre way, Amin's ham-fisted policies had done us a real personal favour and enabled us to get to know a much wider range of people than might otherwise have been the case.

There was swimming, dining and dancing at the Kampala and Entebbe hotels, picnics at Nabinonya, parties at neighbours' homes and visits to local bars. All the time we were receiving worried messages from friends and family in England. "Is everything all right? Are you safe?" We were having a ball.

There were occasional problems, but not due to the actions of the governing régime. On one memorable occasion Rogan had a frightening asthma attack and had to be hospitalised and put on oxygen.

Then there was the episode with Charlie! He was the Congolese boyfriend of one of Jeanette's colleagues and a musician at the Lake Vic Hotel. He had been to visit us and asked if he could give the boys a ride on his motor-scooter. I cannot think of us agreeing nowadays, what with all the emphasis on health and safety, but things were much more relaxed in those days and we readily agreed. When they had not returned half an hour and then an hour later, we were not feeling quite so easy-going. After driving around locally and finding no trace of them, we headed off to Entebbe to try to find Charlie's home. We had no address, just an area of town. When we finally tracked them down, there they were having a wonderful time drinking Coke, eating local snacks and entertaining Charlie's neighbours. They were quite oblivious to our panic of course.

Our pleasurable life should not mask the horrors of what was going on in the country though. The ordinary people were great, but that cannot obscure the tragedies that filled so many of their lives. By 1974, we hardly knew a family that had not been affected in one way or another, especially through disappearances and killings (though they were largely one and the same thing). Economically, things had gone to pot. The factories and large agricultural estates had been run by the expelled Asians and those who were chosen to take over had neither the experience nor the training to be able to run them. Similarly with the shops, many of which had been handed over to army cronies who lacked both the ability and any interest in running them. They sold off what stock they had; and that was that. We learned to queue for beer, sugar and washing powder. So much for Amin's "mafuta mingi" (plenty of oil) campaign. It was a farce.

Time to Move on

We soon reached a stage where we had to decide whether we should sign a contract for a third tour, or whether we should finally return to England. In the end three things conspired to make the decision easier than it might have been. First of all, everyday life was certainly becoming more difficult. Then we had to think of the boys' education. Nick was well installed at Lake Victoria Primary School and Rogan was happy at the neighbouring nursery school where he had the "honour" of appearing on stage for the Christmas production alongside one of Amin's children and with one of his wives next to us in the audience. Nevertheless we needed to think long term.

The clincher was my studies. I was pursuing an Honours degree course and I had little confidence of getting a decent grade after just three years of correspondence studies. When I was offered a place at St Clare's Hall in Oxford to be a full-time student for my final year and promised a good grant to help me to do so, it made the decision (allied with reasons one and two) relatively easy. If it was planned correctly, we could be back home in time to be able to watch the final stages of football's World Cup!

Sorting out a date and getting the flight booked was the easy bit. Then came the eternal round of the ministries to get the paperwork sorted. It seemed to take over our lives. Once again we regularly met the contrast between the uncomfortable facts of life under the ruling regime and the thoughtfulness and kindness of ordinary people. We lost count of the number of times that we were entreated, "Please come back when he has gone." At that stage, we certainly intended to do so.

Finally all the formalities were completed, our packing case and suitcases filled, and we were again booked into the Lake Victoria Hotel for our final two days in Uganda. Little did we know that it was going to be another thirty years before we were to be in Entebbe once more! They proved to be two wonderful, exhilarating but exhausting days. There was hardly a waking moment when one friend or another was not with us to make their farewells. We were all going to be very different people the next time that we met the Ssentamus, the Ssemakulus and Brother Anthony. Our check-in was two o'clock in the morning, and it was a real party time with over thirty friends and colleagues seeing us off at the airport. Never to be forgotten.

By now very few flights were using Entebbe airport and our plane had come via Nairobi, and was already packed with travellers. Just how loaded it was we had not realised; until they weighed us together with our baggage. They were truly on the limit as far as weight was concerned. We did not relax until we were fully airborne and far beyond the shores of the Lake.

And Now For Something Completely Different... ...living life to the full

Chapter 10
Back to England

Eight years in Africa was a significant break in terms of UK career prospects. Things were bound to be very different, not least as there had been a massive shift from the grammar/secondary modern school system prevalent at our qualification to one of comprehensive education. An additional change had been the raising of the school leaving age to 16.

Even taking all that into consideration, teaching plans were going to be put on hold. I had been accepted at St Clare's Hall in Oxford to complete the University of London B.A. studies that had been started at Kisubi by correspondence. After four years of "overseas service", the offer of a post-graduate grant made things financially possible, especially as Jeanette was about to start her long-term position at St John's Primary School in Heaton Mersey. Nick and Rogan were settled in at primary school in Offerton.

I arrived in Oxford without any lodgings sorted out - how naive was that! - but was quickly directed to my home for the next nine months. I was to share a room with an American student, Art Pettee. It worked well even though we were two very different people and he was much younger than me.

Although it was three terms of hard work, it wasn't without its lighter side with new student friends - nearly all younger than myself - relearning the pleasures of real ale and regular games of squash with Tony Lurcock, one of my tutors. Oddly, several of my Oxford teachers were not totally new to me as they had been my tutors during the correspondence course days.

The year ended with the challenging 10 three-hour exams in 5 days (the weekend was free) at the University Examination Schools. It was all over at midday on the Tuesday. A group of friends were waiting at the Turf Tavern. I have no memory of how many pints were sitting on the table awaiting their demise. Suffice it to say, they were well and rapidly consumed.

Whilst on leave after leaving Zambia, I had done a course in ESL (English as a Second Language) at the International School on Shaftsbury Avenue in London's West End. The idea had been to find out what I should have been doing for the previous 3 years. The teaching was not really relevant to that, but did give a good and enjoyable grounding. I was offered and turned down posts in Japan & Saudi Arabia (they would not pay for Jeanette and the boys to be with me), and was considering another offer for Oran when the Uganda offer trumped everything.

There had followed some leave-time supply teaching. First there was a term at Bredbury where I gained experience in what was then called the remedial department. It was a strange few months as there were consecutive teacher strikes during the period, first by the NUT and then by the NAS. As a member of neither union, I had to be in school throughout which enabled the honing of skills in darts, snooker and table tennis. There were a final few weeks at Hazel Grove High

School where I was called upon to teach "remedial" technical drawing. All I could think of doing was to help the pupils to produce scale drawings of football pitches. Thank goodness Uganda called before the boys totally lost their minds.

But now ..... having been Head of English in three African schools and newly boasting a 2:1 degree in English Literature, I was full of confidence for the future. I soon learned that this counted for little. Starting back at the bottom of the heap like a newly qualified teacher was the only option. Teaching ESL seemed a sensible way to go. At one interview, the panel had no idea what that meant and had just presumed it was a mis-typing of ESN. I turned down their job offer, but was then happy to accept a post at Central High School for Boys in Longsight, Manchester. In those days Belle Vue Zoo was still thriving and it was a strange experience to be able, from the upper floors, to watch the giraffes and zebras strolling around. Back to Africa indeed!

This was the start of the longest period that I ever stayed in one school, although Jeanette's experience far outstripped that with her 20-year spell at St John's.

In addition to providing language skills, the intention was to advance my pupils' integration into school life once the basics had been learned. This was a new concept at the time and was not helped by having the ESL classroom in a prefab apart from the main school building. Soon however, the process of getting these boys into mainstream lessons started to bear fruit.

The majority of my pupils were from either Pakistan or Bangladesh. The war leading to independence for the latter country had occurred only a few years previously and far too often it was a struggle to stop the children re-enacting it.

One boy in particular remains in my memory. He was a newly arrived young Pashto speaker originating from the mountainous lands bordering on Afghanistan and who was deeply traumatised. His loneliness was compounded by being the only speaker of that language in the school as it was a regional tongue spoken by (at that time) no more than 10% of the population, and so he could not even communicate with the other Pakistani boys, the majority of whom were Punjabi speakers. After some 12 months of intensive efforts to bring him out of himself - during which time he showed no sign of understanding a thing - we were close to admitting failure. Then suddenly he blossomed. He may not have spoken, but he had taken everything in. Suddenly he was a star pupil. Everything, all the efforts, had been worthwhile. It was a very special time for him, for his family and certainly for his teachers.

It was at this stage that the African sequence of coincidences came to haunt me once again. I walked into the staffroom and heard an unknown voice. Well, not unknown at all really. It was truly incredible that Dick Davies, my Deputy Head in Zambia and whom we had then bumped into in a lift in Kampala had joined us in Manchester as a temporary supply teacher.

Eventually the time came when I had to consider where my career was going. Headmaster Ralph Smith had given me one small promotion step, but without leaving classroom work that was as far as ESL career opportunities could go. But then …. Bob Simister, Head of what was still called the "Remedial Department", decided it was time to retire. My experience in that field had been limited to those brief forays into leave-time supply teaching, but I decided to give it a go and somehow managed to talk myself into the job! The downside was that Bob's Number Two who had expected to walk into the post never really forgave me and understandably that led to a few difficult moments.

A first task was to rename the department as Learning Support, an initial attempt to show that I envisaged a different approach. The school at that time was on two sites - Kirkmanshulme Lane and Daisy Bank Road - a mile apart - which offered both logistical and organisational challenges.

How far we had got when Manchester reorganised its secondary education provision in 1982 I'm not sure, but big changes were clearly inevitable as we were to be formally linked to Moss Side's Ducie HS. We were to become Ducie Central High School, now on three separate sites. I was appointed as Head of the Special Needs Faculty which once again led to some initial human relations problems when the former head of department at the Moss Side school was appointed as my deputy. Happily this problem didn't last and we were to become close friends with Gordon Schofield and his wife.

There was an amazingly diverse cultural intake. I used to joke that a third were white children, a third Asian, a third Afro-Caribbean and the final third from around the globe. The Moss Side riots occurred during this period and we often listened to weary boys telling their stories of what they had witnessed during long nights.

The bright new start began to pall after a while as both the Faculty and I began to feel less valued than had been the case under the previous management. Working with colleagues across the city, often through the auspices of the Teachers' Centre at Didsbury, clearly showed how patchy the provision was from school to school. I became aware that I was becoming more and more negative towards developments at Ducie Central.

That negativity was not helped by the onset of M.E. which blighted everything (not only for me but for the whole family as well as work colleagues) to a greater or lesser extent for a good ten years from the summer of 1984 onwards. The illness was a mystery at that time and had been nicknamed "yuppie flu". My problems were initially diagnosed as stress-based until I heard my doctor quietly exclaim "Oh my god" when looking at some test results. "Go home and wait to hear from the infirmary", he told me. Nick was driving because with my swollen joints I could hardly walk let alone operate the car's pedals. A few hours later, there was a knock on the door which I opened to admit a specialist from Stepping Hill Hospital. "I must be dying", I thought - the NHS doesn't operate that fast except in dire emergencies.

Clearly (and happily) that was an over-reaction! The problems were intermittent, but didn't help my negative attitude towards work. Somehow a new start was needed.

That came when not only did the University of Manchester accept my application to study full-time for an M.Ed., but M.E.C. agreed to second me on full-pay. It turned out to be a wonderful year, both educationally and socially within our small group. Professor Peter

Mittler and his staff also helped in providing the tonic that was so badly needed. It was a privilege that too few teachers are able to enjoy. I firmly believe that a year away from the chalk face should be available to all teachers, not just the lucky few. It was certainly a case of both work hard and play hard. It was a bonus that the study required for my Dissertation took me into every Manchester secondary school to investigate the variety of ways provision worked across the city, and to meet such a wide range of committed colleagues.

Another and unexpected bonus was that one of our study rooms high up in the university's education department looked down on the school, and almost into the classrooms where I should otherwise have been working. An occasional smile at this irony was certainly called for.

Although newly enthused, it was still time to move on to a new challenge. For a while I was, so it seemed, part-time teacher and full-time interviewee. To be fair, I enjoyed that experience travelling around the country to both mainstream and special schools as well as being considered for administrative posts. One was clearly beyond me, others went to the "devil we know" (two of which were rapidly re-advertised) and two I turned down as what they were expecting was unachievable.

Finally I accepted a position as Head of Learning Support at Smithills School in Bolton. It also included an oversight of ESL and a commitment to support the needs of exceptionally bright pupils. Once more part of the brief was to change the culture from having children with learning difficulties taught in a dedicated classroom to integrating them into mainstream lessons.

The only downside during my 5 years there was the recurring M.E. problem. It was a challenging but enjoyable post, both professionally and socially. Added satisfaction came from setting up the local branch of NASEN (National Association for Special Educational Needs) and acting as its Secretary and newsletter editor. Sadly, my periodic absences from school put too many pressures on colleagues who had to cover for me, and early retirement came to be the best solution for everybody.

And Now For Something Completely Different... ...living life to the full

Chapter 11
From High Lane to Argentina

In 1912, my Grandfather, William Mills, was 22 years old, and living at the Horse Shoe Inn in High Lane where his father, also called William, was the licensee. Unfortunately William junior was starting on the health problems which dogged him throughout his life and which eventually led to an early death in 1940.

Medical advice was that he needed to move somewhere with a warmer climate, more conducive to his recovery. The solution was to lead him and eventually his family on an adventure across the world.

At the time, he was employed as a clerk with the Great Central Railway which had international connections with the Central Argentine Railway Limited. In order to support their employee, they informed William that this latter company was recruiting ten or twelve young men who had English railway training for the Chief Accountant's department.

He was interviewed at their London headquarters on 12th August 1912 and immediately offered an appointment as an auditor on a three-year contract at a commencing annual salary of £150, which would rise to £200 when he had passed an examination in the Spanish language.

He was provided with a travel docket to Southampton from where he sailed on the R.M.S. Arlanza. After arrival in Buenos Aires, he was posted to Rosario, a large city and port 300 km north-west of the capital and situated on the River Parana. It was also an important railway centre. For the two years that he worked there, he had accommodation in a large square off the Calle Entre Rios, an impressive street with beautiful colonial buildings and where most railway employees were housed.

But when war broke out in 1914, William felt that he had to do his duty. He sailed back to England and returned to High Lane in order to sign up in the army. Given his original health problems, this might seem a long journey that was bound to fail. And fail it did; but not for the same reason. In this case it was a sight problem that resulted in his being turned down. He also failed to gain employment in the army pay department.

William was told that, as he had been given special leave, his contract in Argentina was still open but he was advised to leave England no later than 28th December. However, his long journey had not been for nothing. Instead of serving in the armed forces, he married Sarah Cadman from another High Lane family. The ceremony took place at High Lane Parish Church on December 24th 1914.

The newly-weds had little time to sort out their affairs before sailing to Buenos Aires. It was not to the city of Rosario that they went to live this time. Starting on 17th January 1914, William was appointed travelling auditor for the railway company; this time he was based in the small pampas town of Venado Tuerto, which had been founded in 1881 by Irishman, Eduardo Casey. The town's name means "the one-eyed deer".

There was a substantial expatriate community in the town and life is likely to have been very pleasant.

Society was centred on the railway, on cattle rearing and agriculture. There was a polo club and William was introduced into the local masonic lodge.

Unfortunately, health issues were again beginning to cause problems; the Argentinian climate had not brought about the hoped-for solution. The decision was taken to return once more to High Lane.

Before their departure, however, Sarah had become pregnant and their son, again (in the family tradition) named William, was born in Venado Tuerto on 13th January 1916. This William was my father and he embarked on the journey of his lifetime on board the R.M.S.P. Demerara when he was only three months old. It was a long and difficult journey, as their ship had to take a circuitous route home in order to avoid German u-boats.

The family continued to live in High Lane. After the Horse Shoe, they had lodgings in Bank House by the canal across from the Bulls Head pub. Finally they moved onto Carr Brow where the house was named Venado. I had always wanted to find out more about my family roots during this period and often talked about going there. However, it was not until February 2009 that we were able to make the journey.

We started out with a short stay in Buenos Aires and as chance would have it, a friend from St Lucien was working there at the time. I emailed: "It's been a while Françoise, what about a drink together?"

"I'd love to Keith," she replied, "but I'm in Buenos Aires."

"So are we," we told her. Our introduction to the town couldn't have been better, with meals out with her and her friends.

But it was our visit to Venado Tuerto that brought to life something of our family history. We left the Retiro bus station in the capital at six o'clock in the morning on what was known as the "milk bus"; not only did it stop at all the formal bus stations along the route, but at every wayside junction where someone had booked to get off. And that is why it was such a tiring six and a half hour ride.

In Venado Tuerto we were supported by Adelaida, a most helpful lady from the municipal council who helped to bring everything together for us. She and the Director of the local museum were at our hotel within minutes of our arrival in town, bringing along a copy of my Dad's birth certificate. We already possessed a booklet in Spanish which we had always thought to be his birth certificate. It was not; it was the civil (birth to death) registration document that follows everybody through life.

After a beer, all we wanted was a siesta; it had already been a long day. Not a hope! People were waiting to meet us at the railway station where Granddad Mills had worked, but first we were expected at the local radio station to do a live interview.

The station where William was based is no longer used as such; the railway industry having all but died there. It is now a municipal office, though they have maintained many of the original features. Just by chance, a goods train passed through, and which our hosts stopped so

And Now For Something Completely Different... ...living life to the full

The radio station at Venado Tuerto

that we could be photographed with the driver! Our welcoming party (about a dozen of them) gave us guided tours of the station and workshop buildings.

Right, I thought! Now for that much delayed siesta - but, oh no, our next stop was at the studios of Canal Ocho for a television interview.

We naturally entertained guests for dinner in the hotel that evening and we were regularly joined by others who had to say how pleased they were to meet the media celebrities. Fame for 24 hours.

The bus from Venado Tuerto to Rosario departed at a much more respectable 9.30 am. We checked into our hotel and then headed off on foot. We quickly found the square on the Calle Entre Rios where William had lived (this was before his return to England and his marriage). The square and surrounding streets are a real mixture nowadays, with the beautiful, old colonial buildings interspersed with demolition sites and very plain concrete constructions. There is still evidence of the elegant life that the colonial inhabitants had built for themselves.

The visit to the old station, Estacion Rosario Norte, where William had worked, was another highlight. Although it is no longer a major railway centre (indeed some of the buildings have been given over to a museum), the size of the place and its elegant wooden roofing on the platform gave an idea of its former grandeur.

By now family history had really begun to mean something, and although that was the "business" purpose of our visit completed, the rest of our stay was equally enjoyable with tours of the capital, visits to both the Argentinian and Brazilian sides of the breath-taking Iguazu Falls and brought to a close with our two final days relaxing on an estancia. Who says that history is dull?

And Now For Something Completely Different.... ...living life to the full

Chapter 12
A Silver Wedding Anniversary Purchase

There was to be no exchange of precious metals. We were going to make a more sensible (romantic?) purchase. A holiday home in France. We had recently taken a short break in Rouen and had thoroughly enjoyed the city itself and the countryside around it. The bonus was that it was near enough to the Channel ports to ensure that we should be able to make proper use of it during the school holidays.

Background research done, a UK solicitor all ready and contact made with French immobiliers, we set off on the morning of the 10th April 1990. A relaxing canal-side lunch with a pint of Marstons at the Malt Shovels in Ashbourne and off to London for the night. The day's real treat was a performance of Sondheim's "Sunday in the Park With George", a show to remain in the memory forever as the Seurat painting is magically recreated on stage.

After a day with cousin Jeff and June at Maidstone and Leeds Castle, we headed off for the big adventure.

The next morning required an early start from the Auberge du Pont in Londinières and then pouring over possibilities (within our price ranges) in the Office of Dubuc Immobliers in Envermeu. Six houses in the day accompanied by Robert Isoz. They didn't give you the addresses and send you off on your own; that might be the way to lose their commission. Really I suppose we should have made an offer immediately when we were in St Lucien where we were royally welcomed by M & Mme Quesnelle. But a good dose of farm-produced Calvados in the middle of the afternoon was perhaps not the best basis for a rational decision.

We had another half-dozen houses to see on the Saturday with a different agent, this time around Dieppe in the Pays de Caux, but really, it was no contest; we had already made up our minds. The next morning we phoned in an offer. An hour later, we came to an agreement. So it was a Sunday visit to the office to sign the compromis de vente that guarantees the sale, and makes things safe for both sides. We put down a deposit which we would have lost had we backed out. On the other hand the sellers would have to compensate us if they changed their minds. Our only get-out was if we could not raise the money to complete.

That was the next task as we had nothing! We opened an account in Rouen with Crédit Agricole who provided a loan to cover the balance of funds needed for the purchase. We supplemented that with a UK bank loan to provide for all of the extras we would need.

Everything was fixed for an August purchase and we drove off to complete the formalities on the day after Rogan's 21st birthday celebrations. We gathered at the office of the notaire, Maître Le Parquier, in La Feuillie for the signing of the acte de vente. The Quenelles were there before us and Mr Dubuc came along to support our fragile French. We learned that both couples had to

And Now For Something Completely Different... ...living life to the full

In the grenier - before renovation

sign every single one of the 15 pages of the sales document - the women in their maiden names. It was explained: you can change partners - there could be a different Mrs Mills next year. Mrs Mills, née Partington protected the woman's rights.

Jean-Pierre & Jeanine Quesnelle came back to the house with us to show us around and then we asked for an appropriate but cheap eatery (after all we had just bought their house) where we could have dinner. They "ummed and aaahed" but eventually decided that the café-restaurant at Morville-sur-Andelle would be OK for the Brits. Cheap it certainly was, but superb value for money; four courses and including aperitif, wine, coffee and calvados for just 52.50 francs. We immediately booked for Sunday lunch!

When we arrived, it was busy. Sunday lunch is an important event in rural Normandy and we could not find our table; but then we realised we had not given them our name. We were led to a window table where the name-plate listed us as "Les Belges". It was obvious that we were not French and English people cannot speak their language. Ergo - we were Belgian. What impeccable logic.

But that is jumping ahead a little. We were rather achy on Saturday morning after sleeping the night on the only "comfort" in the house - the children's old bunk bed mattresses! I crossed the road to the farm where our breakfast milk awaited us in a litre wine bottle. I wasn't allowed to take it home though until I had joined Jean and Denise Pretrelles for coffee - complete with a generous glass of calva! There was a lot to learn about French country living; quite a lot of it alcoholic.

The Saturday was to be dedicated to furniture shopping at Conforama in Rouen. By the end of the day, we had a bed, a bed-settee, a table and four chairs and a small fridge, and the shop would lend us a small van to transport it all. Or that was the idea. No way would all those things go in, so we hired a full-sized van (my first experience of driving a large vehicle through a big city in a left-hand drive vehicle on the "wrong" side of the road). We made it in the end and before we had time to get out of our seats, our new neighbours were there unloading everything for us. They were amazed that it had all to be stored in the garage; we had left the house keys in our car in the city!

It truly was the week of the good neighbours. Jean-Pierre arrived early on Monday morning, to invite us over for a meal later in the week (that was to be another adventure; the six-hour lunch) and to show us the wonderful market at Buchy. Before that I confessed that I lacked the tools to put together some of our new furniture. Should I have done that? Before I could squeak a protest, he and Jean had set to and done it all for me. I truly was a spare part. Jean, Denise and their families spent the week hurrying to Rouen and to Forges-les-Eaux to see to the things we needed to make our new existence work. Amazing.

In the middle of all this, Monsieur le Maire came round to introduce himself and welcome us to St Lucien. "My name is Decanter", he solemnly informed us. "When I was a boy at school they called me Carafe!" We later learned that he had never revealed that to anyone else in the village.

In and between and after all this we did enjoy the beautiful summer weather and started to scrape and paint the shutters!

And Now For Something Completely Different... ...living life to the full

Chapter 13

Football and all that

My love of football goes way back to early childhood. It must have started before I was six, which was when I was taken to my first match at Stockport County in 1948. In those days, I was convinced that I would be good enough to "make it"! Countless children have had that same dream since forever, and probably more so nowadays when television has made the game so ubiquitous and wages have become so outrageous.

The hero of the 1953 Stanley Matthews FA Cup Final cemented things. That is when I bought his coaching kit. Practise, practise, practise; do it enough and I'd become my hero. It is amazing that our house survived the never-ending impact of ball against wall. But even if there had been 30 hour days and eight day weeks, it was never going to happen. At school, I always played for the house team, but never the school team.

There were no junior leagues in those days and so groups of us put teams together and, walking from town to town, would arrange our own matches at weekends and during the school holidays. No referees, no official organisation. Half the time, the opposition didn't turn up but that never stopped us.

At the heart of everything, there was always County. That first match as a six-year-old was in the old shed in what is now the Cheadle End. The day remains more vivid than the match, of which I remember nothing ......

except my first impassioned yell of "penalty ref." Did he give it? I have no idea.

After that, I became a regular, taken along by friends of my Mum and Dad (neither of whom had any interest in the game). We used to meet up in the back room of a family haberdashery shop on Castle Street and I spent many happy hours as a little one pushed up against the front wall on the Popular Side. Those were the days in the 1950s when a crowd of 10,000 was not an unusual event.

As I got older, I was able to go by myself; the 27 bus from Marple to Longshut Lane, down the passage by Birkett and Bostock's bakery yard, and a quick check on railway engines down the pathway on the Booth Street bridge. Yes, I was a train spotter and was able to watch for passing engines from the mound between the Pop Side and Railway End during some less than enthralling passages of play!

After the match I used to run all the way down to Mersey Square to get the bus back to Marple so, as a little one, I didn't have to join the fans queuing on the A6. When I was older, I boarded the North Western bus excursions to away matches there. The journey added to the adventure, particularly so when one memorable day we nearly missed the match. The bus driver didn't know Halifax so asked the way to the football ground. It was not until we got to the rugby league stadium that we discovered that folks there had a different definition of football! We eventually got to the Shay and I remember vividly Ray Drake all but breaking the net with one of the fiercest penalties that I can recall.

And Now For Something Completely Different... ...living life to the full

The County players of the 1950s were my heroes. I thought that they were simply the best. I could never understand why we failed to gain promotion with Jack Connor (my all-time hero), and such brilliant players as Ken Hodder, Bob Murray, Frank Clempson, Trevor Porteous and the rest of the team. At the start of every season in August, I just knew that this was going to be our year!

Becoming a teacher reinforced my love of the game. My first post was at St Anne's C. of E. secondary modern in Newton Heath. It was a tiny school with only 130 children - and half of them were girls (there were no girls' teams in those days). So I did not have a lot of choice for my two teams. If you could run and kick, you were in. That being said, we had some pretty decent youngsters. I remember particularly Joe Makin who went on to sign youth papers with Oldham Athletic, until injury curtailed what could have been a promising career.

My two years at St Anne's were where the refereeing started. In those days the teacher running the home team had the responsibility for "taking the whistle". It is probably just the same today. Also our Headmaster, Frank Briggs, officiated in the Manchester League.

The Zambia Years

When our careers took us to Zambia, I had the responsibility for the 1st year team at Roan Antelope Secondary School; the senior teams were run by far more experienced and talented people. The first training session that I took charge of still stands out in my memory. The boys played barefoot (still not uncommon

And Now For Something Completely Different... ...living life to the full

in Africa) and foolishly I decided to make myself one of the boys. All was well while we tip-tapped passes around the pitch, but then I made the ridiculous decision to take a corner. It was obvious to everyone that I didn't have the cast-iron-like feet of Zambian children. The resulting agony ensured that I never played without boots again.

Roan United was our local First Division team, funded by the copper mine that made the town of Luanshya what it was. Indeed several of our boys went on to play for them. Emmanuel Mwape, who had been goalkeeper at Roan and later went on to represent Zambia in the national team, presented me with an unusual situation. He had a great desire to study sport at Loughborough College in England, but he lacked the requisite number of "O" level passes. So it was that he came into my class for English Language and English Literature. He was 26 at the time and studying alongside boys very much younger than himself. Not only that, but he was older than his teacher! Sadly, he never achieved his desire. He may have been a talented keeper, but the academic life was not for him.

Football was central to our lives. As well as school teams and Roan United, the staff loved a kick-about. I was the goalkeeper; oh to have had a tiny fraction of the talent of my student. In the dry season, the ground was like concrete, so there were plenty of jars and scrapes. Often the senior boys turned out with or against us. At the end of one afternoon's exercise, the heavens opened. We didn't need the showers; soap and warm rain in front of the classrooms was a much enjoyed option.

And Now For Something Completely Different... ...living life to the full

Just as in Manchester, it was the home teacher who took the whistle; but in addition I was often asked to run the line in more senior games. I just loved being part of the game; and if it was at the Roan stadium, so much the better.

While we were there, Ray Wood from Manchester United came to Luanshya to coach Roan's trio of talented keepers, and the following year Leicester City visited and played the national team. A group of British coaches were allocated to each of the 1st Division teams and Steve Fleet from Stockport County (another goalkeeper) came to Luanshya. Next the West Ham United Youth team (managed by John Lyall at the time) toured and when it was our turn, each of us put a couple of the players up in our homes for the duration.

Was I a good "liner" or was it just convenient to be able to call on Keith Mills to take the flag? That is not for me to say, but whatever the truth I loved it. It all came to a head when a group of us, including colleagues who were senior officials in local schools' football, went to Ndola United's stadium for a regional cup final. It was a big day in the sporting life of the Copperbelt and a big crowd was assured. Zambia's sole FIFA official had been engaged to take the whistle, supported by two Division One linesmen; one of whom failed to show up!

That single event changed my refereeing life. Once again, I was volunteered. A track suit was found and, with a crowd of 5,000 yelling, enthusiastic youngsters in the stand behind me, I threw myself headlong into the match. It truly was a baptism by fire. The referee was full of praise for my efforts. You should qualify, he told me.

As soon as we got back to England, I enrolled on a course with Manchester FA. The date of the exam was 8th December 1969, Nick's second birthday. I was determined to sit the exam despite strong objections from the family, and so after the cake and the presents I set out in thick fog to attain my Class 3 qualification!

On to Uganda

Five months later, we set off for another teaching job, this time in Uganda. The posting was as far away from the capital, Kampala, as it was possible to be, up on the border with Congo and Sudan. Once again I was training the school teams, but on this occasion the nearest opponents were 30 miles away on unpaved roads all the way. Then there was the school pitch! I had never seen anything so big; way bigger than the dimensions sanctioned by F.I.F.A even for international matches. I decided to bring it within those international norms. When our Catholic priest headmaster got back that afternoon, he was furious. "It was there to make the boys run", he fumed in his fractured Italian-English.

First year classes comprised anyone from a tiny 12-year-old to a fully grown youth, occasionally with children of his own, and inter-form matches were interesting to say the least! Officially it was not possible to enter secondary school after the age of 16, but with no birth certificates and with primary level headmasters wanting the best for their youngsters, age was a flexible commodity. One year our eccentric headmaster decided to group the children by height which led to our ironically named Giants team, specifically for the tiniest boys.

The bonus for me during our two years up in West Nile was that I was now a qualified official, albeit at Class 3 level with no experience in controlling adult matches. There was only one other qualified official in the whole district. As my Ugandan colleague was the organiser of Cup matches, I was assigned to control several of the finals, including one with Idi Amin Dada among the spectators. That I was totally unready for such responsibility made no difference, and anyway I was full of youthful self-confidence. For the most part things went reasonably well, especially as on-field indiscipline was a rarity. There was one notable exception.

It was the inter-county Final between Koboko and Maracha; an experience that remains firmly within my memory. The match went well until 20 minutes from full-time. With Maracha leading 3-1, I awarded them a penalty. It seemed fairly routine and was not contested. It turned out to be far from that. Remember, there were no goal nets. Nor was there any way of keeping the crowds away from the goal-line, and almost the entire population of both villages had turned up. You just had to get on with it. Unfortunately for what ensued, a Koboko player had hidden himself among the spectators behind the goal and when the kick was taken, he burst through and stopped the ball from crossing the line. Of course, I couldn't award the goal. The offender was sent off and the kick was to be retaken. The Maracha team were not prepared to accept this; they insisted the goal should be awarded.

They were 3-1 up, the penalty was still to be taken; and they would be playing against 10 men for the rest of the match, but they walked off and refused to play on. It took the village chief and his askaris (the village policemen) a full half-hour to get get things going again. The match ended 4-1 and in semi-darkness; night falls fast near to the equator.

Please come into the village hall for a few minutes, the Chief invited me afterwards. All right, my much needed beer in the local bar with friends would have to wait. I soon realised that I had been invited to a post-match "feast". The village girls came round with bowls of water, soap and towels. This was my introduction to eating rice and sauce with nothing but my fingers, cutlery was not available even for a meal of such importance. As a special guest, however, I was issued with my own plate; the only one in the hall to have one. That was a true honour for the sole "white" person present.

After the meal, it was time for the speeches. "And now," intoned the Chief solemnly, "Mr Referee will explain his decision." It took quite a while too as each team spoke a different language and I understood neither. There was a translator on each side of me turning my words into both Kakwa and Lugbara.

For the next two years at our new posting between the capital Kampala and the colonial centre of Entebbe, there were so many other things on the agenda that football took a back seat. Apart from helping (err really?) on the staff team, that was it. At the end of our African adventure, I did manage to arrange our flights so that we could be back in England to watch the final stages of the 1974 World Cup on television. The timing did not meet with universal approval in the family.

Back In England
The following year I went back to being a full-time student, which did nothing to rid me of the excess pounds gathered over the previous few years of the

"good life". Leisure activities consisted of occasional games of squash whose benefit was offset by a keen desire to relearn the pleasures of real ale, following eight years of Zambian and Ugandan lagers.

Then it was time to go home to Stockport. I registered with Cheshire F.A., got in touch with the local leagues and joined the Referees' Society. That truly was the start of another new life as part of a quite different community. Referees take so much stick that many people wonder why they do it and consider us to be lonely, solitary people. Well, it can feel like that when you are the only official at an isolated ground on a cold, wet February afternoon; but that is the exception, not the rule.

I asked the Stockport Saturday and Sunday leagues to break me in gently and to be fair they were very helpful, but it only took my first 15 minutes on Mellands playing fields for me to realise that if I was going to get any pleasure out of this activity I would have to buckle down and learn a whole new way of officiating. In Africa, you were given respect by right, in England it was going to have to be earned. It was a bottom division match and the, mainly (shall we say) "senior" players mauled me; they had me for dinner. A youngster might have given up on the spot, but I was determined that things were going to get much better.

It was in fact the beginning of many happy years both on and off the field. In my first year, I won the George Page Trophy which the Society awarded to the "top" Class 3 official. All right, I felt a bit of a fraud. Most winners were youngsters just starting out on their careers and I was 34 years old. Starting out at that age meant that

And Now For Something Completely Different... ...living life to the full

I was never going to get anywhere near the Football League even if it turned out that I had enough ability. That would take many years of slow promotions.

What it did do was to give me the encouragement and enthusiasm to go as far as this "oldie" could. I was "chuffed to bits" to get a line appointment at a Stockport League cup semi-final. That year the old, now defunct, Ward Street ground was my Wembley.

I progressed as quickly as was possible; Class 2 in my second year and I achieved my Class 1 qualification 12 months after that. The final assessment match was something to be remembered. It was at Northwich Victoria's old Drill Field stadium, with their reserves playing Rylands. I had never been one of the latter team's favourite officials, so it was not an auspicious appointment, especially after I sent their captain off during the match which had almost not taken place at all. There had been a hard frost and despite a thaw during the day, it was still a bit dodgy in the shadow of the stand, but for me at least it was a good result.

Football began to take over my life; every Saturday and Sunday, as well as for the mid-week fixtures at the beginning and end of the season. The routine had its peaks. After a Final line came middles. Two line appointments at my beloved Edgeley Park were followed by a "middle" on the hallowed turf. Saturday 3rd May 1980 was the date for the Stockport Football League's President's Cup Final between Brinnington Celtic and Edgeley Park Rangers. It should have been a match and a day that I would remember for the rest of my life. Should have been! I had been building myself up for this day all week; butterflies were not the problem

- there were much bigger creatures playing havoc in my stomach. I remember getting out into the "middle" and the toss of the coin. After that it is all a blank. I can only assume that nothing went seriously wrong. That, of course, would have lived with me forever.

The Running Years

In my early days as a referee, I quickly realised that I was not fit enough, even with two matches a week on top of a couple of games of squash. This was when I started running; really the only reason was to be better able to do my refereeing job. Our sons, Nick and Rogan, were young at the time. They were my running partners and saviours during the initial jogging sessions and I was grateful whenever they said, "Dad can we stop for a minute please". Thank you lads.

Slowly but surely I put in more and more miles, eventually running to and from work a couple of times a week; Offerton to Longsight and back, with my school books in a rucksack on my back. Sport had become a total obsession, an eight-days-a-week activity. In the early days, colleagues were understandably dubious when I vowed to run a marathon. Their doubts merely spurred me on.

Probably my biggest mistake was to make my first half-marathon the Otter High Peak at Buxton which had more climbs than I was ready to cope with. Of course I just had to go back the following year to prove to myself that it could be completed less painfully. There followed a whole range of races over a similar distance as well as shorter runs.

Eventually the first marathon came along. It was the 1982 Piccadilly Radio Manchester event. I do not wish to reveal how long it took me to get to the finishing line at Platt Lane. I was totally exhausted and, much as I love a good curry, the smells coming from the restaurants on Rusholme's famous curry mile were more than my stomach could bear following 26 gruelling miles.

Of course the run was also a good way to raise charity money. The inspiration was Neil Cliffe, a remarkable man who had, just a year earlier, been operated on for colon cancer and had then decided to raise money for cancer facilities at Wythenshawe Hospital where he had been a patient. He gathered around him an "army" of runners of all abilities. It was a real pleasure to be associated with this very special man. Even the surgeon who operated on him (Mr Hancock, if I remember rightly), turned out with us. As my mum had had a cancer operation in the same hospital and a colleague had recently died of the same illness, raising money to help Neil's cause was very personal and very satisfying.

In the following year I ran the Piccadilly once again and then came the InverClyde Marathon starting and finishing in Greenock. We made a family holiday of it this time to make such a journey more worthwhile.

But the big event came in 1984 when my application for the London Marathon was accepted. That this effectively marked the real end of my sporting life makes it an even more special memory. Once again, it was the excuse for a family holiday in London. After an early breakfast, I made my way to the start at Greenwich. It must have taken 10 minutes for those of us at the rear of the field to cross the start line, so everybody had to record their own time. The official one was a cruel and inaccurate reflection of your efforts. The slower participants will never be winners in the eyes of the public, but amateur athletes are forever competing against themselves.

It was an enormous privilege to jog alongside the awesome gran, Madge Sharples. She did not start running until she was in her 60s and was 67 when I met her on this occasion. What a woman! She eventually competed in more than 50 events and after suffering from arthritis she entered once more in 1996 at the age of 87. In the meantime she had been fitted with two new knee joints and could only walk the course. It took her 11 hours, but she made it. Such a heroine puts your minor problems and setbacks into true perspective.

Then there was the atmosphere. Of course running past such world-famous landmarks made it so much easier, and the crowds were wonderful. Turn a corner, and there was a jazz band playing. Turn another, and there were the pearly kings and queens urging you on. The toughest bits were through the Isle of Dogs which in those days were like a sad desert, and the cobbles past the Tower of London - oh, what they did to tired feet.

The passage up the Mall and past Buckingham Palace was exhilarating, but then that last stretch up Birdcage Walk to Westminster Bridge seemed longer than all of the 26 miles put together. As I approached the finish, the smile on my face was close to that of the Cheshire Cat (appropriate or what!). The tiredness just fell away in the pleasure of the moment. At that stage there was no way that I could envisage that this would be my last event of its kind. In retrospect though, you have to say, "What a way to go out!"

And Now For Something Completely Different... ...living life to the full

Stockport Referees' Society

Side by side with all this I was enjoying the refereeing and the companionship of the Referees' Society. The Hollywood Hotel on Bloom Street in Edgeley was almost a second home during those 20 or so years.

The heart of the Society's activities lay in the monthly meetings. The wide range of speakers were often a joy: top rank referees, football managers and administrators, journalists, players, et al. It was a delight to meet and talk to Danny Bergara, Bryan Robson, Freddie Pye, Colin Murphy and many, many more. There was coaching advice at matches, videos to watch and discussions with the "experts".

We trained together, enjoyed socials and even played matches; I think police teams and referees' teams gave the most trouble to officials! Our Society quiz team had great success over the years in the annual Cheshire competition on the Laws of the Game. I was privileged to be on one of the winning teams.

I was assured that the role of Assistant Secretary ("it will take very little of your time") would only entail taking the minutes. Indeed! There followed several years as Secretary and several more as Chairman. That is what happens when somebody persuades you to dip your toe in the water; you end up swimming the Channel. It was truly a great honour and something that I will never regret.

One of the most satisfying tasks was supporting Stockport County by providing 4th officials, long before these were supplied by the F.A. We saw it both as a great service to our local club as well as a wonderful way to give valuable experience to our local Class 1 officials.

Indeed the last appointment that I was to be involved in was the League Cup match against Liverpool in 1984. I did not know it at the time, but my several attempts at coming back from illness were set to fail. However, if I had to go out, this was a truly memorable way to do it.

Eventually it became painfully obvious (quite literally) that my days of donning vest and shorts for the range of activities that had defined the previous 15 years were over and that I should have to find new ways of passing my time. There were still ways of helping in the development of my colleagues. So I became an F.A. assessor, standing on a Torkington Park touchline with drenched notebook and pen which refused to write legibly, or freezing on a February Sunday morning at Woodbank. The occasional venue with a covered area in the heart of winter was a real pleasure. One of the regular responses that I received after introducing myself to the home club officials was. "Aren't you rather young to be doing this?" Well yes, but at least I was still involved.

One of the bonuses of being involved in refereeing was that, as an F.A. "employee", there was reasonable access to Cup Final tickets. No, not "freebies;" you still paid the full whack. Until then, I had never been to Wembley Stadium and this opened up a new opportunity which I was not going to miss. I loved these days out with colleagues as much as the match-day experience.

County Again

In the meantime, the torture of being a County fan continued. The late 70s and 80s were not exactly the pinnacles of success at Edgeley Park; but how many years had been? Of course the fact that success came so rarely made it even more exhilarating when it occurred. In 1957, there was the battle of the Hatters in the 3rd Round of the FA Cup when Luton Town, then riding high in the old 1st Division, came to Stockport. We hammered them. What a day that was.

In 1965, we went to Anfield and battered Liverpool into (for them) a lucky draw. Even Jeanette was carried away by the atmosphere. The East Lancs Road was awash that night with hooting horns and blue scarves flying proudly from the car windows. Then in 1978 we came away from Old Trafford with a wholly undeserved nothing after a superb performance in the League Cup. That was more memorable because it was the first time that Nick and Rogan had experienced the atmosphere of such a "big" match in a major stadium.

The County Wembley visits were the real icing on the cake, and though we lost all four (1980s and 90s), we had some great days out. I got to three of them, though by the time of number four we were busy with our business in France and couldn't make it. That was probably the best one to miss as it was a real heartbreaker; even on the radio!

Indeed I missed most of the real glory days, especially 1996-7 probably the most memorable season in the history of Stockport County. That was before we could listen on the internet and the bits I gleaned from radio led to some of the shouts and shrieks I made surely audible on the other side of the Channel.

And Now For Something Completely Different... ...living life to the full

At Edgeley Park

And Now For Something Completely Different... ...living life to the full

Chapter 14

Taking Early Retirement

For 10 years, starting in 1984, my ill health had caused me to suffer from physical pain, and mental anguish. My family and work colleagues all suffered from the inconvenience of picking up the pieces during my regular bouts of illness.

I can honestly say that, throughout this time, I had never for one minute considered the possibility of early retirement on health grounds. Each attack was an isolated event which I just had to get over, and then it was back to work. What is true is that after all those years, each return was proving harder than the last. Partly it was guilt: the feeling that I had let down the people for whom I was responsible, causing them extra workloads; partly it was the fear of having to get started yet again.

Then one day, over a drink, someone asked if I had ever thought of calling it a day and applying to leave the profession once and for all. Well, no, up to that point I had not. When I was well (most of the time), life was busy: at work, with the Bolton branch of NASEN (National Association for Special Educational Needs) which I had been instrumental in setting up (with two colleagues, Kath Crowther and Shelagh Smethurst), and with various leisure activities. Life continued to be very full, despite the (on average) twice yearly setbacks.

The seed once sown however started to germinate and with the help of Mike Kehoe, the Head Teacher at

Smithills School, I started to investigate the possibility. The medical reports were so unambiguous that it turned out to be a relatively simple exercise.

Our problem was that eight years service in Africa meant that we had both lost eight years of our pension entitlement (both teachers' and retirement) and that even with the enhancement that was due following medical retirement, we would have a shortfall in our income. That would be so even if Jeanette continued to teach.

What to do about it? I was open to ideas on how I might still continue to generate an income in order to maintain our living standards, but I was not going back as a supply teacher. I had met many retired teachers who had done that, and it was not for me. I had put my all into teaching and had enjoyed it, but I wanted a clean break.

The solution was obvious when we thought about it. We had taken our holidays in France for many years, before eventually buying our rural retreat in the tiny Normandy village of St Lucien. For four years, we had gone there during every major holiday and half-term break and we loved working in the garden and improving the property, but most particularly the relaxed life we enjoyed with our neighbours. Aperitifs on the lawn in summer was the rule not the exception.

Indeed it was those neighbours who had first raised the idea. "When you retire," asked Denise, "will you come to live here?" At the time, it seemed an odd question. It was only later that we discovered that this was just what many people with second homes in France did. Often they lived in rented apartments in Paris and bought a "maison de campagne" for weekends and holidays.

And Now For Something Completely Different... ...living life to the full

They then had a place ready for them at the end of their working lives.

Therefore with my lump sum and (following Jeanette's "escape") the sale of our Stockport home, we could renovate the "atelier" and first floor "grenier" and move into the bed and breakfast business. Simple!

I was told that I could leave at Easter 1994 but I decided to stay on for the first two weeks of the new term. We were due an OFSTED inspection and I thought I owed it to myself and to my staff to be there for that; for good or ill. And I had agreed to do one last play at Stockport Garrick. So the delay was decided upon.

The inevitable round of farewells was sad, but it was also an exhilarating time. As Bolton representative for NASEN, I made my final journey to London for the national assembly meeting. The Chairman gave his thanks for the work I had done and then confirmed that I was leaving the meeting early to return to Stockport to "tread the boards". That was a last night to be savoured. Then there was the Referees' Society; after 20 years as Secretary and Chairman, that was another big evening. Then came the school and NASEN "dos".

The first of these had been flagged up on the school noticeboard as FOOBOM. Fortunately our inspectors did not understand that it meant ""F... off Ofsted, bugger off Mills." A fitting epitaph. Happily, it was worth staying on for. Learning Support ended up with a glowing report. Now we know why you are leaving at this particular time, said colleagues. The only way from here is down!

The biggest surprise in the second was the leaving party attendance of my nemesis from the town hall; the education official in charge of special education. Our contacts had always been, shall we say precarious, as our objectives seemed to be diametrically opposed. Someone whispered to me, "He's only here to make sure that you are really going!" He must have been keen as he contributed to my gift.

And Now For Something Completely Different... ...living life to the full

Chapter 15
The Call of the Boards

For some years the theatre became a central part of my life both as participant and spectator, but it all came from very small, hesitant beginnings. My only acting memory from primary school years was having to arrive on stage declaiming, "By my beard ….". Said beard had come unstuck in the wings but I had to enter, without any facial hair, still loudly pronouncing those now meaningless words. At grammar school, the nearest I came to putting on a performance was as a regular participant in the Debating Society. It wasn't until the 5th form that I had a couple of small parts in "Hamlet"; all very small beer.

As a student in Sheffield I was involved in the annual History Society Review and might have remained on the periphery if, in the final year, the "leader" and principal writer of the material had not got himself suspended for some misdemeanour. The rest of us met together and decided to go ahead without him. We had a couple of sketches and songs, but that was it, and there was much to do if the show was to go on. I cannot recall how it happened, but it was somehow assumed that I would take the lead in organising and writing material. In the end the show went down well and I found that I enjoyed the plaudits that came our way. It felt good and was possibly the spark that lit things up in later years.

In 1965, as an English teacher at St Anne's C. of E. Secondary School, I found myself with the responsibility of putting on a play, this time the Christmas production. It was only a small school, but everybody chipped in with their help, and it was a roaring success. It was not until the curtain came down on the only performance that Frank Briggs, the headmaster, informed me that if he had realised in advance that it would be so good, we could have done several more evenings. Thank you for your confidence FB.

The Learning Years - Luanshya

However, it was during our years in Zambia that I really developed a deep interest in and love of theatre, both at school and at the Roan Antelope Dramatic and Operatic Society (RADOS). My first task was to produce a school play. We chose "This Is Our Chance", a West African drama. It was not great literature, but it gave a chance to portray traditional society and had colourful costumes to distract from any weaknesses in the production. We decided to enter it into the schools' section of the Zambian Arts Festival. We diligently cadged props from everywhere including from the local branch of UNIP, Zambia's governing party and then begged a bus to get us to Kitwe for the competition. Thirteen schools took part with an all-in trip to Lusaka for the national finals as the prize. It was disappointing when we only came fifth, even though two unofficial adjudicators placed us second. Sadly they did not count.

Two weeks later we put it on at Roan for an invited audience and soon afterwards came the bombshell. I was peacefully reading the newspaper one morning when I came across an advert which informed the world that Roan Antelope SS would put on "This Is Our Chance" at the Lowenthal Theatre in Ndola under the auspices of

And Now For Something Completely Different... ...living life to the full

the Theatre Association of Zambia (TAZ) in a week's time. Nobody had thought to inform us of course and, as we were now on our half-term break, a period of massive panic set in, though all went well in the end!

All in all it had been a great experience. We were definitely going to build on what we had learned, ready for the 1968 one-act festival. Given that Luanshya is a copper mining town, I wanted to do something that was considerably more relevant and cutting edge than the previous year's generic production. I found a Scottish piece called "Hewers of Coal" by the playwright and poet Joe Corrie, and adapted it into a copper mining drama which we renamed "The Price of a Dead Miner" and which explored relationships in the immediate aftermath of an underground accident

We were able to breathe life into it because of tremendous support from both within and outside the school. Roger Casalis de Pury whom we knew from RADOS was inspirational, particularly with advice about mining and its terminology and for the loan of props. Not only did he take all of the cast underground to get a feel for things, but we were able to record many of the sound effects while we were down there. Within the school, my colleagues were brilliant, especially Wally Myburgh who took charge of lighting and Peter Cox on set construction. This in itself was quite an achievement. Using cotton sheeting, we reduced the stage to a mining gallery and all of the action took place within this confined space.

The all-boy cast was superb. We were placed second this time. I was distraught; ours was by far the most professional and relevant production, and I had set my heart on going to Lusaka for the finals. I was not mollified when the adjudicators confirmed my judgement privately. I was furious that the team that had worked so hard to put together such a professional production had not won because it was considered too adult for a schools' event. I was told that we should have entered it into the adult competition which would have been a more appropriate setting. Balderdash!

Before this we had both become more and more involved in RADOS. Jeanette helped on props and I was involved in set construction for "Laboratory" produced by Tessa Casalis de Pury and starring her husband. This was the impetus needed, and I auditioned for the RADOS TAZ Drama Festival entry, Thornton Wilder's "Our Town" in which I was cast as Mr Webb, the newspaper editor. We performed at Mufulira's Little Theatre on 28th and 29th May 1968. How we were placed, I have no memory; which certainly means that we did not win. Despite this, it was a wonderful experience and we returned to Luanshya for a short run at the Little Theatre.

My only other opportunity to "shine" in front of the Luanshya public fell through when the leading lady in a two-hander we were to put on ("Murder for the Asking") dropped out. The only remaining thespian opportunity before we left Zambia was to be the 1969 schools' festival. Unfortunately, we were to leave in August and this was not scheduled until late September! What to do?

The decision, backed by my faithful colleagues, was simple. As my "swan-song", I would organise a festival of my own. Why not? Even though I would not be directing on this occasion, it was a thoroughly enjoyable experience. Once again Roger Casalis de Pury stepped up to the plate and agreed to adjudicate for us. Six plays were presented by five local schools in the Roan Antelope school hall over two nights. It was a great way to go out.

Stockport Garrick

There was something of an acting hiatus for three years, but when we had settled back in Stockport, Jeanette and I went to watch a play at the Garrick Theatre, officially the oldest "Little Theatre" in England. Over a pint after the show, we got talking with the society's then President, Betty Pearson, and the play's Director, Joyce Hipkins, both of whom were influential over what followed. By the time we left that evening, I had a "bit" part in Sean O'Casey's "Juno and the Paycock". It was the perfect way to become a member and become acquainted with many of the other members.

There followed a casting as Pozzo in the studio production of Samual Beckett's "Waiting for Godot". This was performed in the bar lounge, where I had to fall down (quite literally) on the feet of the audience.

After that, for some twenty years until our departure to France, the Garrick Theatre became a second home. I was aware that compared with some of the other actors, I had no great talent, but I like to think that friends and colleagues helped me to develop to a reasonable standard. I stage managed, acted and was a member of the House Committee.

I performed as Caswell in Rattigan's "Cause Célèbre," as Wood in Simon Gray's "Otherwise Engaged" and as Dr Paul Travers in Brian Clark's "Whose Life is it

Anyway". Then there was Giles Lacy in Daphne du Maurier's "Rebecca", probably the worst miscasting I ever suffered. A group of pupils from Central High School came to see me as warder in "Count Dracula" and it was subsequently accepted that this role was virtually the same as my day job in the classroom. Among the highlights was playing Nocella in Eduardo di Filippo's "Filumina" which was a real ensemble piece brilliantly put together by Director Joyce Hipkins, and Simon Bent's "Prick up your Ears", the story of Joe Orton.

Nocella

And Now For Something Completely Different... ...living life to the full

Following John Osborne's "The Blood of the Bamburghs", the whole adventure was rounded off by Stephen Poliakoff's "Playing with Trains". Everyone knew that it was my swan-song, and were particularly thoughtful during the run; it was very touching. The only concern was that on the day of the last night, I had to be in London for another final performance as Bolton's representative on NASEN's General Council - would I get back in time? We need not have worried. True, I had to leave before the end of the meeting, but I was beautifully waved off by the Chairman who explained that I was "treading the boards" that evening and offered best wishes for us for our new life in Normandy. What an exit!

In addition I was Stage Manager for three major productions. The first was Brendan Behan's "The Hostage". This was followed by George Farquar's "The Beaux Stratagem". The set had to be changed so many times during this piece - and with the curtains open throughout - that "props-girls" and ASM's had to work in costume. Two members of this team found it difficult to forgive me; Nick and Rogan, both in their impressionable teen years, were not exactly enamoured at having to don tights and appear thus dressed before family and friends. The third one was a real happy romp for "Charley's Aunt".

Perhaps three of the most memorable plays of these years should be left until last; for three totally different reasons. Mike Harding's "Fur Coat and No Knickers" was a delightful scream throughout the run, but what really made it unforgettable was the final (extra) night which we put on, using a makeshift stage, at Quaffer's

And Now For Something Completely Different... ...living life to the full

Night Club in Bredbury. It was a dinner performance. Following drinks in the "library", we put on Act One. The main course of the meal followed and then so did did Act 2. Act 3, following dessert was an hilarious experience as, by this time, the audience had taken on board a more than ample sufficiency of alcohol. I suspect that by now we could have stood on stage and done nothing, and the laughter would still have rolled around us.

For a truly traumatic experience, my part of Mishkin, the postman, in Neil Simon's "Fools" marked a true low. Rehearsals took place during a difficult period of my life. I had been experiencing dizzy spells which were making my sporting life problematic, on the football field, on the squash court and, most worryingly, during a long training run when I found myself unable to run home. A neurologist put it down to stress, but then I developed pains and swelling in the joints which my sports physio put down to a spinal problem for which he prescribed massage with little evident improvement. Part of the play involved a silly Russian dance which concluded with us all falling onto the stage. By dress rehearsal, two members of the cast had to lift me to my feet again; I was no longer able to do it on my own.

Even worse was to follow. By opening night, I had developed a temperature of 102°F (39°C). Throughout Saturday night's performance I lay on a sofa in the dressing room except for when I had to be on stage. The Director begged me to carry on until after Monday's performance, so that he had time to learn my part thoroughly. I was then persuaded to come back for the final night. And although it was deemed a success, it

And Now For Something Completely Different... ...living life to the full

was the last time that I left home for two months! To my regret, I had to drop out of a production the following season because of a recurrence; I had really been looking forward to playing the part of the Manager in "Piaf".

If "Fools" marked the lowest point in my Garrick years, "The Railway Children" marked the high spot. I was cast as Albert Perks, a part that had been made famous by Bernard Cribbins and was both a challenge and a delight. The whole cast, including the children, was a pleasure to work with and the set was another Garrick triumph. A train chugged back and forth across the back of the stage and hidden bodies turned it round on numerous occasions during the evening. One of my tasks was to pull a signal box lever causing the set to miraculously change. A number of audience members were taken in, and wanted to know how it worked.

My final appearance in Stephen Poliakoff's "Playing With Trains" was performed in the midst of getting ready to move to France and perhaps it is not surprising that until I recently reread it, I had no memory whatsoever of either play or performance. It remains a total blank.

And in such a way the curtain finally came down.

And Now For Something Completely Different... ...living life to the full

Chapter 16
Making the Move

But before that...

It was clear that we should need additional income after the early retirement but with no going back into the classroom. We decided on a jump into the bed and breakfast (chambre d'hôte) business at our French holiday home. A whole new world was there to be explored and all in a foreign language; organising the permis de construire (permission to build) with help from the village maire, Pierre Decanter; seeking out estimates from local builders; looking into practicalities of the business with Gîtes de France. And that was all before we had even made the move in the Spring of 1994.

We would be eligible for a grant to help with the renovation costs. This was in support of tourisme verte (rural tourism), but was only available to residents. Jeanette had been refused an immediate early retirement package, so the decision was made for me to live there alone to oversee the work.

To report that things went smoothly in the early days would be stretching the imagination more than a little. The computer blew all the electrics in the house, the lawn-mower handle snapped off and racing around trying to buy a new car was just the start. Jeanette was going to take our Citroen back to England and sell it following the May school holidays. But then the earlier problems became no more than a slight preamble when, one Saturday morning, the BX (locally referred to as the "beex") went "pouf" outside the post office in Forges-les-Eaux; the engine noise was horrendous. The breakdown man gave me the gallic shrug as he gently delivered the bombshell - it needs a new engine monsieur! He couldn't do it anyway as he was off to Tunisia on holiday!

The idea had been that Nick would come over with Jeanette. He would drive her Daihatsu Domino back and she would drive the BX. Recalculations had to be made quickly. Taxis, then hire car provided by Green Flag covered me until we could make arrangements for the Peugeot I had signed to buy the day before the breakdown - more complicated than anticipated as I needed a carte de séjour to get the registration sorted; and that meant a race down to the Préfecture in Dieppe and time to sort out all the necessary paperwork. My brother Kevin said he could fit a reconditioned engine at a fraction of the price of a new one, and Green Flag agreed to repatriate the BX to enable that to happen. The last I saw of that car was as it was towed onto the ferry with Jeanette nervously at the wheel. She then returned to the north of England in the cab of the breakdown vehicle!

There were also plenty of good times. I had found an interim part-time job teaching English to French ladies at a language school in Rouen. The boss's wife was great in advising me on a totally different style of teaching. Unfortunately, her husband's organisational ability was appalling - I wouldn't be staying there very long. I was starting to repaint the whole of the outside of

And Now For Something Completely Different... ...living life to the full

the house and I blew my first week's wages entirely on the purchase of a pressure paint spray. That was better - good progress and glorious weather.

By then I had started to receive visits from builders prepared to do the work. We had decided on four upstairs bedrooms and a visitors' sitting room. It was not difficult to decide to accept Dan Flavin. His quote was reasonable, he was easy to get on with and he spoke English which would make life much easier. An added bonus was that his wife, Annie, is French and was able to intervene brilliantly when things got complicated. The downside was that they lived in Montreuil-sur-Mer in the Pas de Calais and they would have to stay in St Lucien for four nights a week.

By the end of summer, I had finished the painting and Dan Flavin was getting itchy. He wanted to start the work, but we were not allowed to do so until we had received the grant offer (French bureaucracy!). Then came the good news; we had been awarded 78,000 francs (about £5,500).

November 1994 - let the work begin. Dan had bought a caravan for two of them to sleep on the field and two more bedded down in our living room. I had first to clear the empty cider bottles from the grenier and cave; 420 of them. I could see the curtains twitching down at Nolléval as I unloaded yet another boot-load into the skip! I could imagine their minds working: that was some party!

A great advantage of them living on-site was that they put in so many extra hours of work. Those French workmen knew how to drink - but of course! One evening I made the mistake of joining them. Beers in Buchy; wine with dinner and then down to La Petite Vitesse at Nolléval for a glass or two of Calvados.

After that, I joined them no more than once a week for the after-dinner imbibing and board games at the bar. Our draughts champion, let us call him Pierre to save his blushes, did not turn up for work one week. A telephone call to his wife told us that she had banned him! He had been married straight out of school and had never had the experience of going out with the lads. He paid for his share of the rounds at the café which meant that he had to explain to the "boss" where some of his earnings had gone! Keith Mills did not feed him enough, he reported, and he had had to go out and buy extras. When she learned the truth, the proverbial hit the fan and he was (temporarily) refused permission to go to work. Believe me - it is true.

Jeanette was still teaching in Stockport and whenever Dan came up with a new idea, it had to be agreed by telephone. A long-distance marriage the workmen smiled, that must be the modern way. I had to go on a course with Gîte de France as part of the grant arrangements; well that was another way to build on my rudimentary grasp of the French language.

Ceilings and floors were ripped out. New beams and chimney pipes were fitted, as was the insulation. New septic tanks and drains were installed - it was a typically wet Normandy winter and the amount of mud was horrendous. A staircase was made to measure; it was no longer necessary to go up into the grenier by means of a ladder! Velux windows went in the roof, as well as a new full length window door in one of the bedrooms. I was told that this was called a belle voisine (a beautiful neighbour) as that is where she would display her charms to the admiring gazes of passers-by. Dan's brother flew in from Ireland to get the plastering done in double time. He would take one of the workmen upstairs with him after dinner in the evening, just to do another "little hour".

It was a period of intensive effort. The work only started in November and we wanted to open for business at Easter! During the hectic activity, we had an emergency call from our farmer neighbour Denise. Please come across and help "tirer le veau" - that is pull on the rope to help a cow give birth. That was quite an experience for a "townie", and the new-born little one was named Jeanette in recognition of the effort.

Another learning experience was the need for me to feed 4 or 5 workmen; two meals a day for 3 months - a good if nerve-wracking way to learn the arts of the kitchen. I truly thought that I had made it when one of the men asked me to translate a recipe into French for his wife. I whooped and phoned Jeanette to gloat; little did I realise how many more hard lessons there were to learn before I could cook dinners for holiday-makers.

Dan and his team kept to the schedule and by February I had started decorating the whole place. My regular dreams during this period comprised of blizzards of white paint. The downside was the governors at St John's refused to allow Jeanette to leave at Easter; that would have to be delayed until the end of the summer term.

And Now For Something Completely Different... ...living life to the full

The next job was to get the licence to serve the petit-déjeuner. The Préfecture directed me to the mairie at Sigy-en-Bray and they in turn sent me into Forges-les-Eaux. All to be allowed to serve coffee and fruit juice for breakfast! The carpets had been laid, the car park set up and now we had to get the furniture moved from Stockport. The movers were brilliant and by the 5th April all was done.

We opened for our first customers on 10th April. We started with two honeymooners, colleagues from my teaching days at Smithills School. What a way to begin - especially as it coincided with our own wedding anniversary! Pierre Decanter, the maire, donned his tricolor sash for the ceremony and formally declared us open! An exhilarating start to a new life.

The Official Opening

A week later Jeanette returned to commence her final term at St John's - strangely she went on a return ticket, officially travelling from Dieppe and then back again. Bizarrely, this cost only a quarter of the single price!

And Now For Something Completely Different... ...living life to the full

Chapter 17
The France Years

Happily, as I was on my own, the first year's business was fairly light. I had a limited range of dinner menus, and this year gave me time to build up the repertoire. Jeanette eventually made the move in the following summer and we began to settle into a new way of life. We were financially stretched in the early days - at least until the house in Stockport was sold. We had gone from a mortgage and two salaries to two mortgages and only pensions.

Of course this eased in time. We both did some private English tuition around our dining table and the business perked up in the second season as our advertising began to make a difference. Under French law, and because we did not have a restaurant licence, we had to dine with our guests. This was often a delight and led to some life-long friendships.

In these early days social life centred round aperitifs on the lawn; both our own and those of our neighbours. It was one of these evenings that led to the naming of our house. Denise Pretrelle, being her usual joyful self, pointed at the electricity lines, spotted some "spacers" or whatever they are (I haven't a clue), and shouted, "Look, four birds!" And so "Les Quatre Oiseaux" was born; out of a joke.

On another occasion, when a large group of us were socialising in their garden, a passing farmer was

And Now For Something Completely Different... ...living life to the full

Les Quatre Oiseaux

persuaded (much against his will of course) to join us for a "glass" despite his fear of the reception he would get from his wife when he returned home late for dinner. His dilemma was solved when Monsieur le Maire wrote him a formal excuse: "Madame, please excuse the lateness of Pierre. He has been participating in an important meeting to discuss the erection of traffic lights in the centre of the village." This was in a tiny community where two tractors at lunchtime were considered to be a traffic jam!

Next our permanent household started to expand. First of all came Klovis, our rescue collie. "Bonjour Lassie," grown men would call as we walked around town. Then he was joined by our donkey, Cipo. Until recently, our neighbours had grazed their heifers on our field, but when they retired we needed to find a new way to keep the grass down and trim the hedges. Pay somebody to do it? Buy a tractor? Acquire a donkey? It was no competition really.

And Now For Something Completely Different... ...living life to the full

Mario Cipolini was a sprint legend in the Tour de France and as our new four-legged friend was born on the day that Cipolini won a stage of the race into Le Havre, his name was guaranteed. He was regularly photographed by our cycling fanatic visitors. Only 9 months old, when he arrived with us, he cried for his mother through the night. Donkeys are social creatures and he needed a companion. A friend found Utah for us, a large goat, offered by an American who named all his animals after U.S. states. In the early days, we were able to shut them in their shed at appropriate times; until Cipo decided that the wooden door made an appropriate dietary supplement. He was subsequently granted free access at all times.

One thing we discovered was that every animal we had would escape sooner (usually) or later. One new year, we returned to England for a short break. Jérémy, the little boy next door, agreed to feed Cipo in our absence. It was only after our return that a neighbouring farmer told us that he had found Cipo at one o'clock on New Year's Day morning at the cross-roads 2 kms from our home. Fortunately he had a rope in his car and towed the runaway back to his field. I had harsh words to say to Jérémy about leaving the gate open, but at a later date, we were woken by a loud knock on our bedroom window while we slept. Panic! Cipo had got out again and was devouring Jean's cider apples. I told myself off on this occasion. Later I discovered his method of escape. I was in the garden and watched him lean over the gate to the outside and slowly unfasten the bolt with his teeth. Legend has it that donkeys are unintelligent creatures. That is very far from the truth.

And Now For Something Completely Different... ...living life to the full

And what about the freezing pipes? The first occasion was again when we had spent new year in England. We got back to discover that we had no water. Thank you Jean, we thought, for turning it off at the stop-tap by our front gate during a particularly cold spell. This was a winter when the temperature regularly dropped to -20°. It was only at 6 o'clock the next morning when Jeanette reached out of bed to pick up her housecoat from the floor that we found that it was covered with water which was gushing through the bathroom ceiling. I raced next door and opened the sitting room, only to find another waterfall cascading down in there. Two leaks! Two lots of flooding.

Thank goodness for the house insurance and for the presence of Dan Flavin, our builder, when the assessor came along. He got more out of him than I could ever have done with my limited French. On a second occasion, we were open for business and had customers booked in for New Year's Eve. This time, a gap in the insulation had allowed the pipes to freeze. Concerted efforts with the hairdryer failed to solve the problem; not surprising really. Luckily our friendly neighbourhood plumber came out and fixed the problem. Our guests were amazingly understanding considering that one room had a damp carpet and all three couples had to share one washbasin and one toilet. We slept in the "danger room" that night, though "slept" is probably the wrong word as we regularly got up to check for the possibility of more disasters!

A smaller hiccup occurred when our living room fire glass was smashed and needed replacing. Get it done privately we were advised; it will be much cheaper and no VAT. The man smiled and calmly informed us that the cost would be 300,000 francs. The word gobsmacked does not do justice to my feelings. That was about £35,000 - as much as we had paid to buy the house! Thirty minutes later, I was sounding off to my dentist who just burst out laughing. Relax, she said, he's talking old francs; divide by 100! So: £350. Old francs had gone out of circulation 35 years earlier, but many country folk still used their values.

Life started to take on more of a routine. We began to feel more like locals than holiday-makers. The business began to grow. I did the bread-run every morning; 7 kms there and 7 kms back to La Feuillie for the fresh croissants, and then cooking for up to 10 people round our dining table in the evenings. There was a lot of gardening to provide the fresh fruit and vegetables so much appreciated by our visitors. The summers were non-stop, but we had much more free time in the off-season. We could rebuild old friendships and start up new ones, and go to dinners in the village hall. One of the events that we never missed was the old folks lunch; a free feast with plenty of alcohol for everyone in the commune who had reached the age of 65.

Pierre Decanter reported that he had never been to England and asked us to take him. We booked into a B&B and took him for dinner at The Cock in Uckfield. There was linguistic chaos; translating the blackboard menu into French and then forgetting where I was and confusing the staff by ordering in the wrong language. When the landlord heard that Pierre was mayor in a village of only 150 people, he almost collapsed in disbelief. And Pierre had to write a message in French on the pub notice board. A truly convivial evening; which was added to the next day over lunch in a different hostelry. We sat throughout conversing in French, though of course (correctly on this occasion) I ordered in English. "Stop!" called a couple of fellows leaning on the bar as we left. "We don't understand, you are French, but you speak with a Manchester accent." We smiled and left them to ponder on that one!

Our French was still pretty basic during the early days, and so when I read a letter from Gîtes de France offering "free" money to put towards a project to encourage rural tourism, I could not quite believe what I was reading. I raced next door for Anne to confirm that, yes, that was the offer. We immediately developed a project! The garden was extended (taking away some of Cipo's field) and a pétanque court and a tiled garden chess board installed.

The Workload Develops

The next major development was the extension of the kitchen. The original was a bit crowded when we were cooking for 10 people a night. We put in our application to the authorities and arranged for Dan Flavin and his merry men to come along once more to do the work. He could start on the next Monday he told us. Panic! It was Thursday already and we had not got the relevant permission. Don't worry, Pierre assured us. He was going into the office that afternoon and he would see to it that the papers were put to the top of the pile. Six o'clock came round and along with it Pierre, ready for aperitifs and flourishing the signed agreement; we could start immediately. The benefits of having the maire as a friend! The final benefit though was what we always claimed was the secret of a successful marriage; we now had a kitchen sink each!

As my experience of the French language grew, I was asked more and more to do translations from French into English. One very testing early experience was when a local notaire asked me to translate a legal document into English. No sir, I had to say, I cannot do it while you are looking over my shoulder! There was a lot of work too from local tourist boards (I ended up on the committee of one of them).

Then came a phone call from an Asian lady with a second home (a château indeed) nearby. Our GP had promised her that I would translate her husband's hospital discharge papers. Thank you Dr Tahon! Still, it had its upside, including possibly the best curry dinner that we had ever eaten (they brought their chef with them from Pakistan). It took us a while to realise that the daughter-in-law they referred to who had died was in fact Benazir Bhutto, the country's former Prime Minister.

Le Chaudron

As we approached the end of the millennium, we began to feel the pressure. During the high season, the work was unremitting - dinners, cleaning, shopping, gardening. It was a seven day week, 7am to midnight job; just the two of us - no staff. Could we keep the good life rolling and give ourselves a bit more free time? We decided that, if we cut our chambres d'hôtes business down to just two rooms and replaced the revenue with a self-catering cottage, we could have the best of both worlds. Let the search for a new property commence!

In the end, we were lucky and found an ideal cottage in a hamlet attached to our own village - Le Grand Mont

Alix, just 2 kilometres from our front door. There was an initial hiccup when a friend and neighbour unknowingly put in a bid for the same property. But when that was sorted out, we were able to get on with the renovation. It was a big job and much of the place had to be gutted and rebuilt. It was also necessary to reroof it. Until then it had been covered in rusted corrugated metal sheets. We toured the area and eventually found our target; a batch of 300-year-old tiles that had come off a dilapidated old farmhouse. Their colour was gorgeous, much more attractive than the modern copies.

The advantage for Dan and his team on this occasion was that that they could live in while they did the work. Despite its condition, water and electricity were already connected. We were ready to open in time for the 2003 season and once again Pierre Decanter donned his sash to do the official opening ceremony. The next stage of our adventure was under way.

Le Petit Musée Mills

An unexpected development from the acquisition of Le Chaudron - named after the enormous cooking pot which was given to us by Pierre and which we hung in the kitchen fireplace - was the inauguration of my little museum in the outbuildings. Visits to foires-à-tout (car boot sales) and antique shops had become a core leisure activity. In addition, for a couple of years we bought a whole range of antique clocks which went to a friend back in Manchester who renovated them, sold them on and shared the profits. It was a tiny venture which brought in more pleasure than income!

Of course we periodically picked up bits and pieces for ourselves and these began to overrun the house. Hence the value of those outbuildings. In the vaulted cave à fromage (cheese cellar) under the living room, I housed my collection of beer, cider and milk bottles; both French and from the N-W of England. The main room in the outbuilding housed a range of farming equipment. Central to this was a tarare agricole, a large hand-driven machine for separating the wheat from the chaff. The central room became the farmhouse living room with its dominating fireplace. The building had originally been a bread oven for the hamlet. The third room, never totally completed by the time of our departure, was converted into a bedroom, with an 18th century child's metal cot at its heart.

The collection was for pleasure, not intended for the public, but of course we spent quite a lot of time giving tours to customers, friends and neighbours.

I have written about Les Amis d'Ouganda elsewhere, but perhaps here is an appropriate place to record one development. It was a regular occurrence for visitors who had taken dinner with us to telephone and ask for recipes. I gave them out without a second thought. There was no secret. This went on for several years until a regular customer suggested that I should write a cookery book. At the time, I greeted the idea as a joke. I had had no culinary training and had done no more than cater for small groups of holiday-makers. Despite this, the idea took hold and slowly but surely "Dinner at Les Quatre Oiseaux" took shape. It was personally satisfying, but more than that it earned us a reasonable income for our developing charity.

Following our return from Uganda, Mum and Dad joined us on European family holidays on an annual basis and continued to do so after our purchase of Les Quatre Oiseaux. After Mum died in the summer of 1999, Dad came over to stay with us quite regularly. It was amazing how he and Pierre got on like the veritable house on fire, considering that neither understood the other's language. When he learned that the diminutive for William was Bill, Pierre called him Buffalo Bill, whilst the French Peter was dubbed Pistol Pete. Together they became famous (?infamous?) as Les Deux Cowboys.

Keeping Healthy

There were downsides of course. We had ended up living in France because of health problems. For our 23 years in St Lucien the French health service cared for me wonderfully. We were truly fortunate in that Jeanette had a very healthy constitution and she did not even meet our local Doctor for many years. I had eight operations (both major and minor) during our time in the country.

It started off with two hip replacements at the Clinique du Cèdre near Rouen. Dr Vié was so very helpful in fitting in with our wishes. A first one in November to allow us to visit England for Christmas and a second in February so that I could be back cooking for customers at Easter. It was the talk of the department as the surgeon came and sat by the patient's bed every evening for his English lessons. This was not long after the Jospin (Socialist) versus Chirac (Conservative) Presidential election and a common question around St Lucien when the villagers questioned the health of the two hips was: how are Jospin (left) and Chirac (right) today.

I had to go into the central hospital in Rouen for an effort test for angina. I was quickly told that I needed treatment urgently and should seek further advice from the cardiologist. I innocently enquired whether that would prevent our visit to England at the end of that week. No problem was the instant reply. Stay in now and we can insert a stent tomorrow. Wow! I had to wait while they found a room for me (I had already learned that French hospitals do not have wards - only single or double rooms).

However, at such short notice, no room would be available until the next day. A bed was available in intensive care however. Would I be happy to be accommodated there? It did not worry me, but when Jeanette came to see me that evening, it almost caused her to have a heart attack. To qualify for being in intensive care, I had to be wired up as if I was there as an emergency patient!

There was a third major health incident. An intestinal blockage became infected and I ended up with peritonitis. This time it was intensive care and a real emergency. If you had come in 24 hours later, it would have been too late, the surgeon cheerfully reported after the infected parts had been cut out. I have to say that, however unpleasant the following weeks were while I suffered the indignity of a colostomy, the treatment I received was superb. After discharge from the clinic, the nurses visited me at home every single day to deal with what needed to be done. Thank you and your staff Sir and thank you ladies.

And Now for Some Things Entirely Different

In 2010, Jeanette started something which neither of us expected to develop as it did. She joined Les Fées Orientales (doesn't that sound far better than Oriental Fairies, the English language version?). What were they doing? Belly dancing no less. Jeanette swore from the beginning that she would never appear in public, but that vow was soon abandoned, to the extent that I used to joke that her performances were costing us a fortune in sparkly bras!

This was a cultural challenge as well as a physical one as she was the oldest member and the only Englishwoman. She was feted as the group's doyenne and their teacher/leader told the audience at an old folks home, after a performance, that she was probably older than some of the residents!

My own step out from the everyday was on a different plane altogether. The village politics had become divisive. A referendum had shown overwhelmingly that the inhabitants of St Lucien wanted to break away from the governmental partnership with the neighbouring village of Sigy-en-Bray. There had been some problems for sure and I initially backed the idea of the breakaway.

However, the more I thought about it, the more I saw it as a false step both administratively and economically. And so when one of the two competing groups invited me to stand with them for election to the municipal council, I enthusiastically accepted.

We were doomed to fail from the start. Although we gained a majority in Sigy, the majority separatists of St Lucien made defeat for our group inevitable. It was a memorable experience nonetheless and one that I did not regret. Especially as I polled more votes than our group leaders - now that was sweet for an Englishman in France!

And Now For Something Completely Different... ...living life to the full

The End of the Adventure

At that stage our life was still fairly settled, but two major milestones in 2016 made us start to consider our futures. The first was that we were thinking of retiring from our retirement work. The following year we would both turn 75 and decided that, at the end of that year's season, we would call it a day. This decision, coupled with the upset of the Brexiteers winning the referendum, made us think very carefully about our position.

In the end it was a combination of the two things that conspired to ensure our return to Stockport. We sold Le Chaudron very quickly; to customers who had loved their holidays there. The next consideration was where we should live after we were no longer welcoming holidaymakers to our home. With just two of us there, we would rattle around like peas in a pod; we should need somewhere smaller.

At the same time fears of what a hard Brexit might do to us became more and more of a serious concern. There were several dangers, but at the top of the list was the risk that we would lose our free healthcare; that and the capping of our pensions would hit us financially. We were incensed that we had been given no vote in a political decision that was to change our lives forever.

If we were to move, it would have to be now or never. It was an age thing, but in the end the Brexit fears made the decision much easier. So - in November 2017 - our French life came to an end. A new adventure awaited us as we massively downsized and had to relearn an urban life back in Stockport. A new adventure was under way.

And Now For Something Completely Different... ...living life to the full

And Now For Something Completely Different... ...living life to the full

Chapter 18

Back to Uganda and Les Amis d'Ouganda

In 2002, we both reached the milestone of our 60th birthdays. The clichés were numerous: the start of another decade; a new beginning in our lives. Whatever it was, it was an event that needed celebrating properly. Something special, but what could that be?

BBC Radio 4 acted as the catalyst with the programme "Journey of a Lifetime". It invited listeners to apply for a £5,000 grant to take a journey, write about it and turn it into a radio programme. Why not have a go and submit an entry? I planned it, costed it, and then submitted it. Of course we didn't get the grant but the seed had been sown.

We were going back to Uganda. We had flown out from Entebbe in 1974 and had never been back. The plan was to visit friends whom we had not seen for 28 years and to revisit places we had loved during our four years in the country.

We knew a great deal must have changed since the dark days of Idi Amin Dada who held sway when we were last there. We had no idea of what to expect. We needed help, so we enlisted the support of Brother Anthony Kyemwa who was headmaster of St Mary's College, Kisubi in 1974 where we had spent our final two years in Africa.

"Yes, of course," he said, "no problem." An ex-student of the school had recently opened some international quality accommodation, The Royal Suites, in a suburb of Kampala. It was on the expensive side, but we booked one of his cheaper rooms. We could stay there for a few days while we worked out our plans. After all, we were going to be travelling "everywhere". But we could sort it all out after our arrival. We still fancied the independent approach; no guided tours for us!

A few weeks before our departure the Radio 4 factor struck again; this time even more significantly. I was doing something in the kitchen; Woman's Hour was on in the background, but I was not really listening. Then there was a mention of Uganda, and my ears pricked up. Kate King, founder of the Dream Scheme charity in England, was talking about several affiliate groups that had been founded around Kampala. They were working with extremely disadvantaged youngsters and they were clearly doing wonderful things in their communities.

Could we do more than just have a holiday, we wondered? Being a pushy fellow, I immediately emailed them and asked whether we might go along and offer support in the form of encouragement. Of course there was little else that we could do. After all, we were only going to be in the country for a short holiday. Knowing what we know now, it was no surprise that our offer was immediately accepted by the local volunteers.

The morning of 2nd December 2002 dawned while we were on Flight BA 63 out of Heathrow. We approached Entebbe on time, but we seemed to spend an unusually long time circling over Lake Victoria. The Captain explained: "We are safer staying up here than attempting a landing!" There was a violent thunderstorm around the airport.

Welcome back, we thought, a normal flight could never be taken for granted. On the occasion of our last departure 28 years earlier in 1974, the plane had been heavily laden and passengers had been weighed along with their luggage, just to be sure. And of course the runway does come to an abrupt end at the shores of Lake Victoria!

We were driven straight to the Royal Suites ("Soots" in local pronunciation). The place had bed-sits and suites; the latter were right outside our budget, even for those first few days, but we were conducted into a palatial set of rooms, complete with its own veranda and garden. There had obviously been a mistake. But, no, there hadn't! As an ex-teacher at St Mary's College, we had been upgraded. It was a luxury way beyond our experience and set the tone for a holiday which was both enormously enjoyable and fulfilling.

One of our priorities was to meet up again with our old friends Charles and Kevina Ssentamu (we had trained as teachers with Charles in Sheffield in the 1960s). It almost didn't happen. Charles had retired from the teacher training college where he had been the Principal and moved to a rural setting near to Masaka. Nobody knew exactly where he lived and all we had was a post office box number. We made the 3-hour drive and after asking around town we had sadly decided that we had failed. It was both frustrating and upsetting that we were not going to be able to meet up again after all those years.

Finally at our last stop, a petrol station where again they had never heard of Charles, a young man buying a soda heard our question and offered to help in our search.

With our new friend we visited some schools repeating our question, until eventually we found ourselves at a boda-boda (motorcycle taxi) stand where we got directions. We needed to take a small murram (earth) road, and turn off by a tree that had been felled by a power saw! Simple. At the turning, I got out of the car to check whether the road was suitable to drive along. As I tentatively ventured down, who should be walking up towards us? You couldn't make it up could you?

It was a joyous but brief reunion as Charles had an appointment. We drove him there and arranged to come back for lunch on the following Sunday.

However our day was not yet over. In the excitement of the reunion, we had almost forgotten our new friend sitting in the back of the car. He was a local Muslim primary school teacher and incredibly it was eid-ul-fitr that very day. He wondered - would we be good enough to join him, his wife and baby for their celebratory meal? What a wonderful day with true Ugandan hospitality to welcome us back "home."

We got to know our old friends all over again, but we also developed friendships with their by now grownup children, some of whom had been born since we lived there in the early 1970s.

We also went back to St Mary's College and spent time with Brother Anthony. We did the Kampala and regional tourist bit all over again. These experiences were hugely enjoyable, but are stories for another place.

For this is the story of the volunteers at Dream Scheme Uganda and how, instead of us encouraging them, they inspired us.

On the morning following our arrival, Jane and William Walusimbi were waiting for us at reception. Jane's first baby was due any day, but that had not stopped her from

In Traditional Dress

journeying across the pot-holed streets of Kampala, side-saddle on the back of their motor scooter.

Much of the rest of our visit was taken up with visiting schools, churches, and Dream Scheme groups. We picked our way through alleys and across foul waterways in the suburbs of Kampala to be warmly welcomed in the poorest of homes. Along with Dream Scheme members, we planted shrubs at a teeming city cross-road.

The visits to Bubebbere, where much of our work is now concentrated, were safaris into what seemed like the end of the world. The village is only an hour's drive from Kampala, but the way (it couldn't be called a road) was all but impassable without a 4x4. Bubebbere is on the shores of Lake Victoria, a 30 minutes trek beyond the last power lines, and it is a "road" to nowhere for even this route goes no further than the small trading centre.

It was no surprise to learn that people saw no reason to stay in the village. There was no future for them there. The vibrancy of the children and the enthusiasm of the volunteers at the Little Angels Primary School was in total contrast to their everyday lives. On one visit the place was full of shouting, excited youngsters who, although it was in the middle of the school holidays, had come in to collect their examination results. They sang for us; they danced for us; we watched a display of gymnastics. It was also prize-giving time. Winners received two biscuits as their prize; runners-up only got one!

It was at this stage, witnessing the contrast between the terrible classroom and home conditions and the joyfulness of these children whose futures were bleak, that we decided that we would have to do something to help. How that would develop remained to be seen.

As for the long-anticipated visits to at least three corners of Uganda, they just did not happen. We were too busy, too happy with friends old and new. There were definitely going to be other opportunities for travel, but after all, people are more important than places.

Back in St Lucien

So what could we do to raise some money to help them at Bubebbere? Just as a one-off event, you understand. After pondering all sorts of possibilities, we came up with the idea of a Garden Party; a very English event in the middle of rural Normandy.

We discussed it with our neighbours; we should certainly need their support - and probably their gardens. They liked the idea, but we couldn't call it a garden party. Such an event in France is only for posh people; in the local parlance, it is very "snob".

By the time June and the event came along, we had printed programmes ready to sell, full of advertisements from local business folk who had generously agreed to support us. We had decided that we needed four gardens, each with a different theme. In one, there was a craft and farmers' market; in a second we had a car boot sale, a bar and horse rides; in the third there was live music all the day long. In ours, there were various stalls, competitions and games; and of course tea and scones!

Most popular of all, we recruited our donkey, Cipo. "Guess the weight of the donkey" went down a bomb, especially as the prize was a bicycle. After all he had been named after a record-breaking Tour de France cyclist! The only problem came when our local vet tried to take him off in his trailer to be weighed at the local farm cooperative. He was not going to get into that thing; who knew where he would end up? We finally succeeded, but all the time he was away, his bosom pal, our goat Utah, cried. She must have thought that she had lost him for good.

The day dawned and the weather was glorious; too hot if anything. There were fewer visitors than we had hoped for, but we nevertheless ended up with 1,000 euros in the pot and everybody confirmed that it was a most enjoyable day.

My reaction? Thank goodness that is over. I was exhausted. Still, it was only a single event, wasn't it? Then came the neighbours' questions? "Can we fix the date for next year?" "How can we improve things and expand the attractions?"

Ah well! If we were going to do it again, we needed to set up a committee, officially register as an "association" and get ourselves a bank account. The one-off event had transformed itself into a permanent part of what we do. Our lives would never be the same again.

By the time of our next visit to Uganda, we were fully registered in France. We were still in the process of sorting out our role, but we were more or less organised, and so in January 2005, Jeanette and I were able to look, in more depth, at what our Ugandan friends were doing to try to help the youngsters in their care. We had been using the slogan, "Helping others to help themselves" and it was clear that the dedicated men and women who were running the Dream Scheme groups truly cared about the children, many of whom lived in appalling conditions. They more than merited any help we could give them.

In addition to checking things out, while there we ran a three-day course on basic healthcare. We had no qualifications whatsoever to do this and we even had two nurses among our "students", but it seemed to go down well and was hugely enjoyable, especially on the last day when we were privileged to be in the audience for the role-play afternoon. This is when they passed on the information to the villagers at Bubebbere. It was hilarious as they played out the health lessons in their own language, Luganda. At the same time we were able to hand over the funds that had been raised over the previous two years. That money was to purchase land in the village which would support them in their aim to become self-sufficient.

Undoubtedly, one of the most significant developments in the work of Les Amis d'Ouganda was the start of our child sponsorship scheme which slowly got under way in the middle of 2006. Given their circumstances, it was amazing that some of the children managed to get to school at all and we decided sponsorship was the best way to help them.

The number of orphans was high, AIDS having carried off so many of their parents' generation. Often they lived with grandparents and when they died, the children could be dispersed far and wide to whichever members of the family would take them. Failing even this option, they had to work while they were still of primary school age. Even the more fortunate ones had work to do, both before and after school; fetching water, caring for younger brothers and sisters, working in the family garden.

Just to get to school could be a real challenge. They had to walk; often several miles. That could be daunting enough, particularly for a six-year-old who is malnourished, but during the rainy season the pathways can become even more treacherous. It is not surprising that they did not always get there.

They also had to find their school fees. By our standards, these are very little, but so often the youngsters turned up at the beginning of term with a chicken or a few vegetables in lieu of money. Often our colleagues accepted them. However, without the fees, there was no money for the teachers' salaries. How do you attract efficient, qualified staff, when there is the chance that they will not be paid?

So the people who started to support one or more of the children were doing more than they perhaps knew. Not only did they provide the children with an education, a uniform and a lunch, but they were giving the two "Little Angels" schools at Bubebbere and Bulumbu a stability and a future. Thus the whole community has benefitted; there is now a focus which makes the village itself more viable.

With help from another donation (nothing to do with us), our friends constructed The Little Angels Children's Home on the Bubebbere campus. Now some of our sponsored children could live in conditions that would give them a greater chance of personal and educational progress. We were also able to support the project with beds, bedding and mosquito nets. Not least however was that we could help pay for the provision of food.

The development of Les Amis d'Ouganda
Now that we were an official entity, we had to consider our approach and our way forward. A year on and the second "gardens" party took shape. It took the same format as the first one with one big addition. As well as the four gardens of the previous year, we had the use of the large property across the road, and there with the support of passionate car enthusiast supporters we were able to have a display of vintage cars.

To be honest though, the amount of work involved for the return seemed disproportionate and was both exhausting and time consuming. Happily Jeane

And Now For Something Completely Different... ...living life to the full

Charlionet a friend/supporter came to the rescue by proposing a balade contée, a country walk with story-tellers and music. With support from the Maire of the neighbouring village of Nolléval and aided by a lovely summer Sunday afternoon, the scene was set for the first of a string of annual events for many years to come. We held it in a different village each year and Jeane, as a story-teller herself, had all the contacts necessary to attract a wide range of volunteer participants.

We were regular stall-holders on a variety of foires à tout (car boot sales) and craft markets and a friend-musician couple later agreed to put on an event in the village hall at La Feuillie. It turned out to be a Tango evening with music, singing and a demonstration from a tango dance group from Rouen.

Naturally we were eager to expand what support we could give our Ugandan colleagues. Over the years, in addition to small grants from banks both in France and UK, we were able to secure finance from French government sources; from both our département of Seine Maritime and from the Region of Haute Normandie. These funds helped with a range of self-sufficiency programmes, with the provision of water for both communities and schools, as well as capital building projects, culminating in the building of the school hall at Bubebbere.

At Bulumbu there was absolutely nothing at what is now a fully-functioning campus. It was a case of starting from scratch. We have become used to attending inauguration ceremonies, all very momentous days for us and the villagers, but the day that we performed the

With the younger Ssenyongas

first opening at Bulumbu in 2007 will always remain in the memory. There was just one single classroom at that stage, but we knew that it was the start of something special.

This is the time to acknowledge another indispensable source of support. I was resting in my hospital bed one evening awaiting an operation the following morning when I received a call from our local insurance agent who told me that he had a contact in Kampala who might be prepared to help.

The Palle Moeller Foundation gave us wonderful aid during the years to come, sharing the burden in the development at Bulumbu. We remain truly grateful for the years of support they gave us.

The construction of the Golden College secondary school was another momentous development. We had been able to support our colleagues' dreams at the primary school level. But what was there for the children after that? A secondary school education was beyond the dreams of all but the lucky few. So George Senyonga came to the rescue. When he first showed us the open piece of hilly land that he told us was going to become somewhere for the village children to pursue their dreams, we thought it was just that - a dream. We were not counting on George's determination of course. He was prepared to do everything for the children. In this case it meant selling up his own business and even putting his home at risk in order to succeed.

Only a few years later, Golden had become a fully functioning school, supporting pupils for six years right through to UACE, the Ugandan equivalent of British A Levels and the gateway to further education. It is so very pleasing to report that a number of sponsored children have been able to use it as a springboard into university and professional lives, while others have moved on to careers in a range of vocational areas.

And Now For Something Completely Different... ...living life to the full

And Now For Something Completely Different... ...living life to the full

Chapter 19

After all These years

As I pen this final chapter, we are celebrating more than 20 years of our work with the Ugandan children. Returning to live in England meant that we had to register with the British Charity Commission and we found that the direct translation of our French name, "Friends of Uganda," was already being used. So what could we call ourselves?

On one of our regular Uganda visits, we were relaxing one evening with Pam Winders who had been instrumental during our early days in setting up in UK. We were looking back at a newspaper double-page spread on our work in the Sunday Monitor, a Kampala newspaper. The headline was "Forever Friends of Uganda." Easy decision! We had been born anew.

Moving back to live in Stockport was a major change for us; a transition from rural Normandy to an urban setting after 24 years of country living. We had both reached 75 years, but once again a new future was opening up for us.

Forever Friends of Uganda

By now the number of trustees involved with FFoU had grown and we were spread across various parts of the country including Northern Ireland, with Martine, our blog manager, the furthest away, living in Austria. This created problems with meetings especially for the AGM and the problem was added to by the Covid lockdown. Luckily Zoom came to the rescue.

And Now For Something Completely Different... ...living life to the full

As the charity grew, and the workload increased, we found that we were having serious problems maintaining communications with our Ugandan colleagues. This became so difficult that it threatened the viability of the charity until James Ssenyonga, son of Dreamscheme's founding couple, George and Berna, came to a timely rescue. He gave up a prestigious career to dedicate himself to the dream, and in doing so he brought new life to the partnership. It was both generous and inspiring, and we were back on track.

Our sponsorship programme continues to be at the heart of what we do, and it is certainly paying off. The number of young people who have been supported from their nursery years, through to university and into successful careers has continued to grow.

It is a true pleasure to look back at the school as we first saw it in 2002, a ramshackle block of classrooms at Bubebbere, and make a comparison with what exists now in the villages - two fully functioning campuses. The development has continued, both with the infrastructure and with what the school can now offer.

Central to the latter was the inauguration of our Abawala Ku Mwanjo (Girls First) programme, the prime objective of which was levelling the gender playing field. The aim is not only to give girls skills but to keep them in school and help them to feel their worth.

During the awful two years of school lockdown during the Covid pandemic, the amount of schoolgirl abuse and the number of pregnancies rocketed. It was at this time that we financed a skills centre at Bulumbu to give those affected the possibility of a worthwhile future if they could not return to school.

And Now For Something Completely Different... ...living life to the full

Other developments included the push to "green" the schools, and the grounds are now planted with shade and fruit giving trees, and the children are involved in growing their own food. The schools also follow a reading for pleasure programme. Too many of the adult Ugandans that I have spoken to see reading as no more than a way to pass exams. They are now learning that reading can be a pleasure as well as a means to improve their future.

Our ultimate aim is to enable the schools to become self-sufficient and the construction of a dormitory at Bulumbu was planned with exactly this in mind. As things stand, the number of paying pupils attending the schools is tiny. The schools' survival currently depends on the sponsorship scheme. If sufficient paying boarders can be attracted, the schools could become financially independent, with less reliance on FFoU, while the Ssenyonga family could continue to offer school places to children in need. At the time of writing, we cannot know how this will end.

Of course any educational success story has to be rooted in academic progress. The Ugandan system demands that girls and boys pass the PLE (Primary Leaving Exam) before they can advance to the secondary sector. In the early days moving up to secondary school was almost unheard of at Bulumbu and Bubebbere. One of the joys of the partnership with our Ugandan friends has been to witness year on year improvement in the pass rate. The money we raise has meant that we can offer higher salaries, and this has attracted better teachers, which has contributed to better pass rates, which in turn encourages more paying pupils. With support from

And Now For Something Completely Different... ...living life to the full

FFoU and its sponsors, tentative steps have grown into strides. There is much more to do, but now there is real hope for the future.

What about Jeanette and me?
As already mentioned, recent years have heralded a big change in our lives. After 24 years in our rural idyll, we have returned to urban living. From spacious accommodation with land surrounding our two houses, we down-sized to a small terrace - though at least there was a pub at the end of our small garden!

Naturally one bonus was that we were now close to our family. We had been used to seeing our sons, their wives and our grandchildren on their occasional holidays in France and on our visits back to England. As Rogan darkly put it, we had come close enough to be cared for in our declining years!

To be honest, it took some getting used to, and not only in terms of space. We were in the habit of having people around the house and at the dining table on a regular basis. It was something that we had always enjoyed, but now it became a much rarer occurrence. Another need to adapt.

We grasped (and are still grasping) the opportunity that having cinema, theatre and restaurants on our doorsteps has brought us and with free transport available, a trip into Manchester has become as everyday as a walk to the corner shop. That possibility has brought a range of pleasures; both cultural and gastronomic.

The Football (Re)Connection
Moving back also meant coming home to Stockport County. There has been the real pleasure in being able

And Now For Something Completely Different... ...living life to the full

to support the team that has meant so much to me since I was six years old. Plus, time spent in the Cheadle End and at occasional away matches with the family is an added bonus.

Even more than that, the County/Uganda connection has been significantly strengthened. Half of our trustees are County fans, many others sponsor the children's education and even more are associate members and donors. Our achievements would have been much less without the County factor.

The Club and individual fans have regularly offered us kit to take with us to help the Ugandan football academy that we have supported over the years. It is a personal joy that, with the support of Steve Bellis, the Club President, the link is being strengthened. We have already had our work promoted at a pre-match corporate meal with a linked double page spread in the matchday programme.

We have also been awarded bucket collections which bring in valuable funds. The most recent and gratifying advance came with the appointment of Fraser Horsfall as a player ambassador.

For me personally, a highlight was my 80th birthday 12.5 mile fund-raising walk that I completed from Stockport Town Hall to Edgeley Park (where we were waved off by staff) and on to the County training ground at Carrington where we were welcomed by the Manager and players with whom we shared lunch.

160th Birthday Party

FFoU was conceived during our 60th birthday celebrations, and this stage of our story concludes with a celebration of our entry into our 9th decade. The plan was to wander down memory lane and then to tentatively look forward to what we could do next!

So the question was. How should we celebrate! Perhaps a special trip away? Or maybe a family meal? Yes that would do it. But that was before the intervention of Rogan and (more especially) Sharon. Such a landmark merited a party. No, we countered. Unnecessary and unwanted.

Happily, the seed germinated and our enthusiasm grew along with it. A whole range of ingredients resulted in an unforgettable day. There was the setting of course. Before our years in France, Stockport Garrick was an integral part of life, and the ideal venue. Then there were the musicians and the catering. Both were excellent, as were the family's inspiring efforts in decorating the hall.

But top of the list must be the guests. To bring together friends and relatives from every decade of our lives and from all the places we had lived proved a dream too far. The celebration lacked friends who wanted to attend but couldn't, and those who planned to be with us but had to drop out for a range of reasons.

But for those of you who attended - thank you all so very much. You made it an afternoon never to be forgotten.

The End... But only for now.

And Now For Something Completely Different... ...living life to the full

Our 160th Birthday Party - Cheers!

And Now For Something Completely Different... ...living life to the full

And Now For Something Completely Different... ...living life to the full

And Finally...

The end, but not yet I hope...

When I started writing these memoirs many years ago, my stated aim was to leave something of our lives to all the members of our family who came after us. There is still so much of my Mum's and Dad's lives that I wish I knew more about; things that I ought to have asked them when I had the chance. Once you've gone, it is obviously too late.

There were occasions when I truly believed that this would never be completed. There were so many times that life got in the way every time I said to myself - we'll get it done this year. Fingers are now firmly crossed that we are finally over the finishing line. To mix a metaphor, the proof of the pudding is in the reading.

A major unforeseen benefit of writing my story has been the chance to relive all the experiences and remember all the people that have filled our lives.

But it's not finished yet, is it? We're still hoping for a bit more and relishing new experiences. Life is still full of interest and challenges:

Forever Friends of Uganda (still the biggest call on my time and emotions). Stockport County and its engagement with our charity work. The support from the Club has been a real delight after 75 years of my support wherever we were.

The family of course, especially now that we are almost on each others' doorsteps (not literally, they will all be delighted to confirm).

Our involvement with U3a (University of the 3rd Age) has also kept us from sitting in front of the fire in our slippers.

Nor have we given up on theatre, gigs, restaurants and holidays to destinations near and far.

In the end, now that everything is finally committed to paper, the memories can live on and will remain even after our turn comes to exit - stage left naturally!

My thanks go out to so many people.

To Jeanette who has had to put up with everything, including my whims, fancies and stubbornness, for a lifetime.

To Fil and Rogan who have helped to improve my writing, chapter by chapter, year by year. To Alison for giving the entire work a final polish.

To everyone who has been part of our story and who helped to make our lives what they have become.

To Merv Payne at Victor Publishing for his help and guidance and then for bringing all the words to a meaningful conclusion.

And finally to all of you who, when I have talked to you about the "project," have said, "I want to read that". I truly hope that you feel that it is worth your while.

And Now For Something Completely Different... ...living life to the full

Got a book in you?

This book is published by Victor Publishing.

Victor Publishing specialises in getting new and independent writers' work published worldwide in both paperback and Kindle format.

If you have a manuscript for a book of any genre (fiction, non-fiction, autobiographical, biographical or even reference or photographic/illustrative) and would like more information on how you can get your work published and on sale to the general public, please visit us at:

www.victorpublishing.co.uk

Printed by Amazon Italia Logistica S.r.l.
Torrazza Piemonte (TO), Italy

54441737R00118